COLLECTED POEMS

THE AUTHOR, 1951

Collected Poems

RALPH HODGSON

LONDON
MACMILLAN & CO LTD
NEW YORK · ST MARTIN'S PRESS
1961

MACMILLAN AND COMPANY LIMITED
London Bombay Calcutta Madras Melbourne

THE MACMILLAN COMPANY OF CANADA LIMITED
Toronto

ST MARTIN'S PRESS INC
New York

PRINTED IN GREAT BRITAIN

EDITOR'S NOTE

This book reproduces the contents of Ralph Hodgson's three published collections of poems : *The Last Blackbird and Other Lines*, 1907 (by kind permission of the publishers, Messrs. George Allen & Unwin, Ltd.); *Poems*, 1917; and *The Skylark and Other Poems*, 1958.

Hodgson has published (so far as I know) only two poems not included in these collections : 'The First Nightingale' *(Saturday Review,* 27 April 1907) and 'Forbid the Day' *(Saturday Review,* 15 July 1911); the second and third verses only of the former poem were published under the title 'The Late, Last Rook' in *Poems.*

Hodgson was born in England on 9 September 1871 and now lives in Ohio, U.S.A.

COLIN FENTON

CONTENTS

The Last Blackbird and Other Lines (1907)

Poems (1917)

ILLUSTRATION

Lines

No pitted toad behind a stone
   But hoards some secret grace;
The meanest slug with midnight gone
   Has left a silver trace.

No dullest eyes to beauty blind,
   Uplifted to the beast,
But prove some kin with angel kind,
   Though lowliest and least.

The Treasure-Box

I WOND'RING see the rainbow stain
  The sea; I dumbly guess
Why on a wintry window-pane
  Late Edens effloresce;

If bubbles at the river's brim
  Have souls for destiny;
Why twilight freights the blackbird's hymn
  With deeper mystery;

If chiff-chaffs voyaging in March
  Are charted by the light
Of angels' eyes whose pinions arch
  A hemisphere with night;

What ocean maids through ocean shells
  Sing ocean roundelay;
What tears are those in evening bells
  A harvest field away;

What gladness fills the yellow wren
  When June is in the thorn;
What triumph knows the great sun when
  A winter rose is born.

The gold-winged exquisites that shine
  Upon the yew in May
But sadness give this heart of mine
  That cannot know their day.

I wond'ring watch the new gnats weave
  Mad mazes in the sky,
And guess their joys as they achieve
  A moment's empery.

I guess the tales on buntings' eggs —
   Who runs may never read —
Drain speculation to the dregs
   About a thistle seed.

I have a crystal treasure-box,
   Its stores are held from me;
I cannot force its thousand locks,
   And have no master-key.

Saint Athelstan

O NOT the rain that wets his face,
  And not the winds that beat and chill,
Not these bid shepherd mend his pace
  To-night across the hill.

It is no sheep hath shepherd lost,
  Yet hoarse he cries, and crying will
He cross again as he has crost
  And crost again the hill.

A strong man's eyes with grief a-swim
Are like to make an angel's dim:
Whose prayers him choke or ever twice
He prays will angels sacrifice
A time of blessed Paradise
    To minister to him.

Then, shepherd, kneel and plead thy care:
  Saint Athelstan will help a man!
  What prayer a weeping shepherd can,
  The shepherd makes Saint Athelstan,
And makes again his prayer.

O shepherd, look! the cup of night
  Is broke, and clouds, dividing, yield
  To thee a sign, to thine a shield;
Look! comes to earth a line of light,
From Heaven it comes and waxes bright
  As Heaven itself concealed.

4

Now hasten whither thou art signed,
And on a pitchy moorland find
  A wide and wild and pitchy wood
  As ever on a moorland stood
With mountain lands behind.

Where pathless lost lands lie away
  Rise mountains gray and banded black
With forests under mountains gray,
  And on gray mountains mountains stack
  And dwindle to a skiey rack
For clouds there fixed as they.

And there's a stony slanting pit,
  And deep a mountain-side it mines,
A crevice in a mountain split,
  And capped with fallen pines.

So deep above the cape is drawn
  No winds come there nor ever sun;
There dusk is ever one with dawn,
  And noon with midnight one.

Lone habitant the cavern hath,
  And lean at eve she stole away,
And gray she picked her secret path
  As ever wolf was gray.

A chilly wolf it is she runs:
  An empty maw's a numbing bed.
  Over the mountain's cloudy head
Climbed, seen or hid, three winter suns
  All since the gray wolf fed.

And on she comes in starving state
To hunt the marsh where last she ate,
And wander, whining, at a loss
To rid her of the weary weight
Behind the rib herself would freight;
To leave the marsh and hunt the moss,
And howl her hunger overcross
A land obliterate.

She's on a bank with willow hung . . .
What news upon the night is sprung?
The gray wolf there, with eyes aslant
And nostril slits agape, gives tongue
And knells, not calls, her want.

What thing is hinted in the wind?
Some wasted hare or sodden bird
Dies in the grass, or feebled hind
Is fallen from the herd?

Nay, none of these is rumoured there;
There is no knowledge in the wind
Of dying bird or dying hare
Or herd-forsaken hind.

But wandered feet have run the wild,
And in the wood are eyes affright;
It is the shepherd's haunted child
Is in the wood to-night.

'Twixt cloud and cloud a small sun shone
And weakly ruled the winter day;
Was shepherd on his labours gone,
The shepherd's boy from home alone
Went, wonder-wist, astray.

The sun fell like a god rebuked,
  And east the lost boy turned, and west,
And south and north the lost boy looked,
  And is the dark wood's guest.

As down the trees the shadow crept
A night-bird through the shadow swept;
  The lost boy heard her evil scream,
And where he stood he sank and wept
  His way to icy dream.

And wakes to see — what sees he there,
  Or is his sense still led in dream?
What tricks with hope his chill despair
  Who heard the night-bird scream?

As were there moon might fade her stream
  With beauty through wet woods and bare,
  Fades in his view a silver stair
Lit by a fading beam;

Lies in his view a fellow-guest
  Irradiant there with gentle light;
Was never mortal vision blest
  With lamb so holy white.

But, lost boy, listen — is it wind
That rustles in the thorn behind?
  Nay, listen — look! O sight all dread!
The lost boy stares and, horror-blind,
  Swoons down upon his bed.

Ay, shepherd crying, louder cry,
And let thy anguish, rising, buy
  New grace for him whom Terror's wing
Hath felled, lest he a midnight lie
  In madding trance, and wakening,
Open an idiot eye.

O shepherd, come into the wood,
    And call and hear and clasp again
    Whose eyes, if weeping, open sane —
Whose eyes have looked on sainted blood
    And seen an angel slain.

Look in the sky, thou favoured man,
    And raise thy joy and higher raise
What praise a weeping shepherd can!
The shepherd makes Saint Athelstan —
    And makes again, his praise.

With holy ruin grass is red
Where in a wood a grey wolf fed:
    The wolf is in her mountain pit,
    And night's a world to west of it,
Day tops the mountain's head.

The grass is red; will rains remove
The hallowed mark; soon Spring will glove
    The wood anew, and none will tell
    The pity of that miracle;
    It will be told where angels dwell,
Its wonder and their love.

The Sedge-Warbler

In early summer moonlight I have strayed
Down pass and wildway of the wooded hill
With wonder as again the sedge-bird made

His old, old ballad new beside the mill.
And I have stolen closer to the song
That, lispèd low, would swell and change to shrill,

Thick, chattered cheeps that seemed not to belong
Of right to the frail elfin throat that threw
Them on the stream, their waker. There among

The willows I have watched as over flew
A noctule making zigzag round the lone,
Dark elm whose shadow clipt grotesque the new

Green lawn below. On softest breezes blown
From some far brake, the cruising fern-owl's cry
Would stay my steps; a beetle's nearing drone

Would steal upon my sense and pass and die.
There I have heard in that still, solemn hour
The quickened thorn from slaving weeds untie

A prisoned leaf or furlèd bloom, whose dower
Of incense yet burned in the warm June night;
By darkness cozened from his grot to cower

And curve the night long, that shy eremite
The lowly, banded eft would seek his prey;
And thousand worlds my silent world would light
Till broke the babel of the summer day.

The Missel Thrush

I s a w the sun burn in the blue,
And a missel thrush flew by,
And the missel thrush to a chestnut flew.

I saw a white cloud in the sky,
And linnets sang — their breasts were red;
And linnets sang melodiously.

And up the sky the white cloud sped,
The wind woke crying in the trees,
And the white cloud battened, his bulk was fed

By a thousand clouds that swarmed like bees;
I heard the rough wind whistle shrill,
And the clouds banked up in billowy seas.

O wild the day that was so still!
The elm flung tribute of her green,
And linnets tossed from hedge to hill.

The sun was gone and the wind blew keen,
The clouds grew gray and grayer grew,
The sun was gone behind the screen.

The wind blew wild and wilder blew,
And shriller screamed and louder bawled,
And spun with fury round the yew.

Like a bruisèd snake the yew branch crawled
And cricked and hissed like a bruisèd snake
Where the sheltering blackbird shrank appalled,

And waking slept and slept awake
And huddled stupid from the day,
Nor heard the clatt'ring thunder shake

The cloud that hung so low and gray;
I heard the thunder shake the cloud,
And the rough wind come and die away.

I heard the gray thrush piping loud
From the wheezing chestnut-tree;
The gray thrush gripped the spray that bowed

Beneath the storm, and brave sang he —
O, he sang brave as he were one
Who hailed a people newly free!

But all was fear and hope was none,
For Heav'n bled flame as Heav'n were Hell;
Still the thrush sang blithely on.

The rough wind sank and the rough wind fell —
O, the rough wind died upon the hill,
And thunder was its passing-bell.

The gray cloud burst, I saw it spill
Black floods as skiey seas fell whole.
The thrush sang with amazing skill;

The gray thrush heard the thunders roll,
And sang and heard not what he sang.
The Storm King claimed a noble toll,

I saw his golden fang,
I saw it close upon the wood
That loud with thrush notes rang.

I looked again: the tempest's hood
Was torn across; I saw the sky;
So green and new the chestnut stood,

The elm lay split hard by —
From bough to bole the elm was split,
And above was melody.

I saw the sky — the sky was lit,
The sky was lit with sun.
I saw a gray thrush by me flit;

He sang no song — his song was done;
I saw his studded breast;
And plovers rose, ten score as one,
And ribboned in the East.

The Last Blackbird

My head was tired; I had no mind to think
  Of Beauty wronged and none to give redress:
I got me to a place where linnets drink
  And lizards go in ferny loveliness.

A blackbird sang, so down I fell; meseemed,
  Soothed by his note, I closed a drowsy lid;
And I was ventured on a dream — I dreamed
  One stood and questioned me how linnets did.

And straight I knew who thus in angel guise
  Would have my news — some trick of lip or brow
Guessed me her rank; I said not otherwise
  Than ill indeed it went with linnets now.

And with the words I got upon my feet;
  Her look said she would hear if I had more:
I led her to an ancient mossy seat,
  And blest the hour for my inquisitor.

'Nature,' I said, 'O thou whose hand controlled
  And ordered chaos to a reasoned plan
With "Know thou me, Old Night, and loose thy hold!"
  And in whose accent Life and Love began:

'Whose "Keep thou this, and thou that circuit go,"
  Or "Here stand thou, and thou in that place stand,"
Lifted a meek or laid a hot star low,
  Chartered a sun or cancelled his command:

'Who flattered with an object aimless spheres,
  And gave to each place, precedence and class,
Time and degree, till constancy was theirs,
  And perfect system where no system was:

'Hear me! The blackbird piping from the hill,
  His insolent wild eye — its yellow rim —
His coaly vest and yellow mandible —
  Is he not thine? Wouldst thou continue him?

'Art thou still minded, Nature, to provide
  The salts and sweets a frolic wagtail picks
Out of the spume that quilts an idle tide
  Behind the trough where meeting waters mix?

'Hast thou a mind to keep a redstart dressed
  As now and heretofore; to order still
Thy system of economy unguessed
  That gives a shiver to his flaring quill?

'Wouldst thou still keep the chiff-chaff to his song,
  And have him know to braid his grassy dome?
Wouldst knot and twist with many a weedy thong
  The green confusion leaping round his home?

'Is still thy mind for wrens and little springs
  And ferns and sudden stoats and popping mice,
And all the myriad noisy rainbow wings
  That make the wood not less than Paradise?

'Wouldst in thy season strip the little wood
  And hap it over with a frozen coat,
To spot a corner there with icy blood,
  And stretch a rabbit with a frozen stoat?

'Hear me,' I said. 'Thy wood's a grandam's tale;
  Its trees are felled; save one its birds are dead;
Thou art unqueened; now other hands prevail;
  One blackbird lives — he is the last,' I said.

14

And she, 'The poisèd moths thy hand caressed,
  Sip they not wines from fuchsias by the sea?
Runs clear no stream to bright a linnet's breast
  Or sparkle in the moon? Nay, gladden me!

'Sure Beauty's in the pine the heron crost,
  Or Beauty's on the heath or down or plain,
Or Beauty's on the yellow desert lost
  In desert glare? Nay, make me glad again.'

I said the place was changed where hawk-moths sipped
  Eve's sugared cup; nor now was Beauty's mark
Upon the stream where once her linnets dipped,
  And moony bubbles raced into the dark;

'Wild Beauty's left the down whereon she lay;
  The heaths and plains are bare; shy Beauty's fled
The woods; fierce Beauty's left her desert day;
  Beauty is fled or dead. Beauty is dead.

'Yon blackbird with to-night will end his race.'
  I stopped, and Nature rose and looked abroad:
She came again and asked who ruled the place;
  I named then him who reigned its overlord.

'Thou madest all things equal under thee;
  To all thy gifts were Beauty, Love, and Youth.'
'I pricked a vein that I might gladden me
  With flower of that my seed thou callest Truth.'

'Thou chosest one not fairer than his kin
  To keep the story of thine eyes' delight.'
'I gave a book to choice of mine wherein
  To chronicle that pleasing in my sight.'

'Who learned the letters equal to his task
   To open ways beyond his right employ,
Who got him to a fiction and a mask
   And hid the book he did not dare destroy!

'Not then he heard the noises in the cloud,
   Nor cried his wonder when the leaf uncurled
After the wind, nor went he wonder-browed
   Adoring when the rainbow spanned the world.'

She said, 'I gave him ears —' 'He waxed them in.'
   'And sight: I taught him beauty was my sum.'
'New gods he found: they taught him sight was sin.'
   'And speech and song.' 'He blasphemed or was dumb.

'On every wind his evil fame was blown;
   His every step struck fear and panic doubt;
Suspect and shunned, he armed and went alone,
   Or with sly wisdom walled himself about.

'He woodman turned and wide he laid his axe;
   Stream, hill, and heath, to all he put his hand,
Taxed pitilessly all; all paid the tax;
   Only the sea ignored his ill demand.

'He saw thy hills and brought a newer plan;
   Hill, stream, and heath he tricked to evil whim;
Only the sea ignored or countered Man,
   Only the sea despised and countered him.

'And soon for sport a hunting he would go;
   The chase is over save for yon last bird
Whose wing to-morrow —' 'Shout me this last woe!'—
   I shrank beneath the angers I had stirred —

'Whose wing to-morrow — shout! This final prize —'
  'Will deck his stony mate for holiday.'
Ten thousand hells roared out of Nature's eyes,
  She pressed her lids and shut the rage away.

'But knows he never midnight questioning?
  Is every sense I gave him dead or dark?'
I said, 'He knows he reigns to-day a king,
  And has forgot the day he was thy clerk.'

'Henceforward is this world his gaud, his toy;
  If bones he wills, in bones the world will lie;
His to deflower, infect, defile, destroy —
  Unless —' She said, 'Thou hast a remedy?'

I said, 'Save one, not I : reject, annul
  Him, seed and breed and story, or have done
And send this world, thy Bubble Beautiful,
  With sudden moth-want whirling at its sun.'

She answered me, 'The last was spoken ill.
  My world is good; its streams may yet run pure;
My blackbird now is piping from the hill!'
  She listened to his lazy overture.

Miraculous old song! Our wonder met:
  She turned away and listened to the bird.
'To-night.' I said, 'to-night he'll pay the debt.'
  'To-night,' I said, but him alone she heard.

'Only the sea!' Then Nature, rising, stood:
  'The chase is over; yon last bird is free.
Before I give new beauty to the wood,
  How say'st thou, poet, to a wider sea?'

17

She looked above: small as a pigeon's wing
　　A cloud came up and crost the blackbird's tree.
She said, 'How say'st thou if yon blackbird bring,
　　To wash my world, a deeper, wider sea?'

I woke. A dizzy man I reeling went
　　Round by the hill: a blackbird hurried by;
Clouds raced and cracked; to some high argument
　　Were hurrying the gossips of the sky.

The Down by Moonlight

THE down looks new whose lonely slopes I climb,
Yet is he old despite the dress he wears:
Old as the dark and concreate with Time,

Waste with the affliction of uncounted years.
A weary head he stretches to the pale
Of Heaven; one bended arm of him uprears

A shaggy fist, as if to turn the hail
And fire of tempest fraught with new distress
For his old brow; and one arm seems to trail

Its atrophied and bony nakedness
Down to the streams that bless the living land,
As if, to mitigate the loneliness,

He too would reach, as we, another's hand.
So quiet this hour is grown, a whisper's fall
Were sacrilege; within me as I stand

Shy wonder, waking, seems a common brawl,
And even thought itself is over loud;
Desire alone is dumb; no plover's call;

And if owls fly, their flight is unavowed
For cry I hear of theirs: peace here and far,
And save the moon's loved presence one lit cloud
Is sole 'twixt me and night's first listening star.

Holiday

I WOKE to hear the song that early rang
My boyhood on from Spring to fairer Spring,
The song of wonder, new as when I sprang

To its first note with boyish welcoming.
O may its glory fail not from my sense
Till Life — the Toll-bridge crost — unquestioning,

With Love alone, in last obedience,
Turns to the Dark; nay, even in that hour
When clay shall merge in final consequence

With clay, whose sod — moist cradle of some flower,
Young heart's-ease blue or blest anemone —
Leaps to the sun, I would remained yet power

In my cold ear to stir the heart of me
To heed if echoed faint such anthem there
As poured at waking from my window tree.
I rose and fed my soul on that sweet fare.

I rose and listened to the wildest lay
Brown song-thrush ever made to song-thrush brown.
The wild song ended and I looked away

And saw the angel Sunshine on the down;
I saw her largen yellow on the green
Wide fields; I saw her slowly sweep and crown

The proudest elm the sun hath ever seen;
I saw her search along the hedge and find
The bluest violet ever sent to lean

A shy face from a too attentive wind;
Deep in the gloried elm the angel found
The mildest dove that for a mild dove pined;

To her embrace I saw a skylark bound,
The loudest lark that ever dared the sun
Or, tranced with bliss, swooned from his own sweet sound.

Where would my angel there a way she won
With melody for half a world and me.
Was never day for holiday begun
Like that a thrush hailed from my window tree.

The Linnet

THEY say the world's a sham, and life a lease
　　Of nightmare nothing nicknamed Time, and we
Ghost voyagers in undiscovered seas
　　Where fact is feign; mirage, reality:

Where all is vain and vanity is all,
　　And eyes look out and only know they stare
At conjured coasts whose beacons rise and fall
　　And vanish with the hopes that feigned them there:

Where sea-shell measures urge a phantom dance
　　Till fancied pleasure drowns imagined pain —
Till Death stares madness out of countenance,
　　And vanity is all and all is vain.

It may be even as my friends allege.
　　I'm pressed to prove that life is something more —
And yet a linnet on a hawthorn hedge
　　Still wants explaining and accounting for.

The Winds

GREAT scutcheoned moths with velvet hoods,
And moths whose wings bore no device,
Blundered out of dusky woods,

Constrained by some rare avarice
Or deeper sense not guessed by me,
To seek in flame their Paradise.

Bleaching fern and waning tree —
Tired of these the willow-wren
Sang and slipped off oversea.

No medalled thrush for music then!
And the blackbird cock made melody
No more than his brindled hen.

Hour in, hour out, the dragon-fly
Raced his image in a ditch
Blue with cloudless undersky;

Or it was Night, then Night was rich
In eyes her own whose downward glance
Found every pool a glass in which

No cloud impaired her countenance,
When Autumn, a reluctant heir,
Came into his inheritance.

And long Night found no cloud impair
Her beauty where, in sun arrayed,
The dragon-fly still came to share

Blue waters with his burnished shade.
But the woodlands sickened surely; now
Never tree but Autumn laid

Infecting fingers on its brow.
Pink with disease and fungus-dun,
A few leaves fell from a sunlit bough. . . .

I watched them falling, one by one —
The self-same leaves that opened new
Without a spot to self-same sun.

There came a time when Night wore through
And saw no moon in pool or stream;
Her steps were traced by dawn that grew

To day beneath a hindered beam;
And the sleepiest elm of a sleepy row
Pawed the wind that cost her dream;

And the woods around, aloft and low,
Fell troubled with many a wind;
Then half the winds came up to blow

With half the winds behind,
And a redbreast sang on a barley-mow
A dirge to a sun gone blind.

O now the rout of leaf and bough!
And O for memories of Spring!
To every leaf far-flying now

Some memory did cling —
The wood-wren dropt on a nearer spray,
His song and his shaking wing —

The thrush — the egg on scarce dry clay —
The thrush that woke before the dawn,
To first discover day,

And the song that came when blinds were drawn,
And the quiet owl-time mapped for me
Upon a moon-washed lawn,

Under a wide-armed tree,
Faery Asias newly sprung
From a green, enchanted sea —

O seemed with every dead leaf wrung
From every branch once green,
And on the tide of refuse flung,

There went a leaf unseen,
From spoiling boughs of memory
Some grace of what had been.

Now far beneath a billow sky
The rape of woods was borne:
No hedge but there went piracy,

No thief but stripped some thorn;
And the bough that gave not with the blast
The closer bough was shorn.

No tree in the pelt of wind and waste,
Sheer to the dint of all,
But seemed of weariness at last

Herself half green must fall,
With twice a hundred thieves to sack
Her ruined coronal.

'Twixt elms across the tempest's track
Tossed one more vast than they;
Her story told a woodland wrack

Spread far as woodland day;
From the measure of wealth her branches bore
No wind that blew but took its prey.

And winds were here in many a score,
Scraping, screwing, gnawing some,
Like rats on a granary floor;

And winds to crawl and clasp were come —
Winds sprung from a serpent seed;
And winds to rive and throttle from

Starved packs of a wolfish breed;
And many a wind could fancy find
Fetched out of hills at eagle speed

To stun and bruise and thrash and grind,
To clout and tug and clip and tease;
And they roared and drummed and blared and whined

And bleated and whistled in fifty keys,
And sighed and howled and sang and mewed,
Winds of divers and all degrees,

A preying maniacal multitude,
Avid as they whose furies hew
A ship into sticks of kindling-wood

A morrow's gentler tides shall strew
Round tearful isles and isthmuses
With an eyeless, bony crew.

Anon, anon, nor end nor ease!
I let Imagination feign
Great beating hearts in wooden trees,

Gave wits and sense to knot and grain,
And saw a heart-broke elm go mad
Betwixt a bedlam twain.

Their leaves a whirling myriad,
Forth Autumn's windy lip,
Fled up a weedy field that had

No tree her tooth might strip;
Some fell and some made haste anew
As slaves that heard the whip;

Then many fell; a far-borne few
Lost now and later seen,
Tossed high above a hedge into

A tree nor red nor green,
And they trickled through her skeleton
Like ashes through a screen.

So Night without a moon came on
A land of sunless day,
Enriching still with carrion

The manors of decay
Must woods and valleys never fair
That skirt the Year's highway.

Dread mists and mildew flourish there,
And tumour-blooms endow
With poisoned sweets the cold, dead air.

Naught of beauty with me now
But, like dead leaves left behind
Staring from a frosty bough,
Would be off with any wind.

My Books

WHEN the folks have gone to bed,
 And the lamp is burning low,
And the fire burns not so red
 As it burned an hour ago,

Then I turn about my chair
 So that I can dimly see
Into the dark corner where
 Lies my modest library.

Volumes gay and volumes grave,
 Many volumes have I got;
Many volumes though I have,
 Many volumes have I not.

I have not the rare Lucasta,
 London, 1649:
I'm a lean-pursed poetaster,
 Or the book had long been mine.

I have not an early Herrick;
 I have wanted Dowland too,
Since that lover of a lyric,
 Symonds, wrote 'The Key of Blue'.

Never has my luck been lashed
 To the Mariner of York,
And in First edition washed
 To my bookshelf: egg of auk

Never was so rare as this
 Volume that earned Dan Defoe
Deathless literary bliss.
 I have not Ned Ward, nor know

That the rhyming knave I want
   Who did such a merry ill
To Don Quixote; D'Avenant,
   Too, I lack, and Aaron Hill.

Books of travel; books of sport;
   Books of no or some or great
Theological import;
   Books about affairs of State,

Absent are with many others;
   I can't boast an early Donne,
Nor the 'Poems by Two Brothers',
   Though I have *a* Tennyson.

But enough of treasures lacking!
   If my cloak is frayed and torn,
I will send King Covet packing,
   And present the cloak as worn.

Are my senses gone asleep?
   Sure I hear John Suckling laugh
From his grave in ancient sheep,
   As, hard by, in mottled calf,

London, 1651,
   Lab'ring Carew once more sighs
Through a score of sonnets on
   Mistress Celia's long-closed eyes.

Comes a rather female song,
   Sweet and sad; 'tis Tommy Moore
Singing of Ierne's wrong
   Just as Tommy sang of yore.

Near him Rogers bitterly
   Wails this oddest freak of Fate's —
Folks, he hears, buy 'Italy'
   Only for the charming plates.

Near the 'Wit's Interpreter'
   (Like an antique Whitaker,
Full of strange etcetera),
   'Areopagitica,'

And the Muse of Lycidas,
   Lost in meditation deep,
Give the cut to Hudibras,
   Unaware the knave's asleep.

There the tinker's won'drous son
   (Lately come into his own)
Urges still the Pilgrim on,
   Shouts again for Mansoul Town.

Written by a friend of Keats,
   That torn fragment next the Clare
Lightly of 'The Fancy' treats.
   Next to Masson's Essays, there,

In three volumes Bagehot lies:
   Wiser pen among the witty,
Wittier among the wise,
   Never wrote about the City.

On the broad back of his race
   Swift, there, cuts with savage art
Half a fiend's, half ass's face;
   Will time ever soothe the smart?

There lies Coleridge, bound in green,
　　Sleepily still wondering what
He meant Kubla Khan to mean.
　　In that early Wordsworth, Mat

Arnold knows a faithful prop, —
　　Still to subject-matter leans,
Murmurs of the loved hill-top,
　　Fyfield tree and Cumnor scenes.

Ayrshire's Peasant-Poet-King
　　Sang his soul into that page,
Stopped — a lark shot on the wing —
　　Just as his Muse came of age.

There is Byron, nowadays
　　Held in small repute by some.
He must do without their praise.
　　And there's Shake — and THERE I'm dumb.

Fauna of my crowded shelves,
　　Birds of an unequal quill,
There they roost like labelled elves,
　　Waiting mine or Fate's last will.

On a day outside my ken,
　　Soon maybe or haply late,
These will pass to other men;
　　One will know a rarer fate.

Book of cloud and wind and sea,
　　More than all the others mine,
Ere the Roll is called for me
　　Knowest what end will be thine?

I will have thee to the fire;
  So thy Parent went his way,
After ocean stilled his lyre,
  From the sands of Spezzia.

In Fancy Fair

FANCY at her garden gate:
Fancy may have long to wait.
Pole to Line and sun to snow:
Fancy may have far to go.

Memory hath dreams: the birds,
Prisoned sobs and passioned words.
In the waking sun they stand,
Life's drab riddle in his hand.

Thrushes, O be silent now . . .
Now with song record his vow.
Shrink not, daisies, as they kneel.
Part they now for woe or weal.

Hope is hers and hers long prayer,
His a loop of her dark hair:
Hope is hers, he'll win the world:
Fancy's sails are wide unfurled.

He will come again at noon,
His bright way with roses strewn.
From the turnpike wave good-bye,
From the hill-top — hope is high!

Wave her wait and wave him well . . .
Memory no more may tell.
Hope is high: O then beware!
Gauds are cheap in Fancy Fair.

Now a gray dream Fancy weaves:
Roses change to cypress leaves.
He lies bleeding, dying, far
In the cloud and wrack of war;

Or in hunger walks and want,
Hope a spent illuminant.
He has sunk (God!), sold to shame
A dishonoured, ancient name;

Or, though victor in the race,
Is forsworn : some fairer face
Lures his soul to Lethe letch.
Mark ye how that grisly wretch,

Wrinkled Doubt, the malice-eyed,
Mad his midnight mare doth ride . . .
Fear and lies and old despair
Haunt the lanes of Fancy Fair.

Face them, Fancy, show thy whip!
Pariahs! each lifted lip —
Each red coward mouth will flee
To the kennels. Comfort thee.

Take new roses for thy breast :
He will dream and come to rest.
In the shadows he will come;
Do thou fend with faith his home.

Slow the deep tear upward wells,
Fancy changing sentinels —
Fancy at her garden gate :
Fancy may have long to wait.

Thrown

I'M down, good Fate, you've won the race;
  Bite deep and break a tooth in me;
Now spit your poison in my face,
  And let me be;
Leave me an hour and come again
With insults new and further pain.

For of your tooth I'll make a pen,
  And of your slaver ink, and will
I bring a joy to being then
  To race you still:
A laughing child with feathered heels
Who shall outspeed your chariot wheels.

The Hammers

NOISE of hammers once I heard,
Many hammers, busy hammers,
Beating, shaping, night and day,
Shaping, beating dust and clay
To a palace; saw it reared;
Saw the hammers laid away.

And I listened, and I heard
Hammers beating, night and day,
In the palace newly reared,
Beating it to dust and clay:
Other hammers, muffled hammers,
Silent hammers of decay.

Beauty Sprite

FALSE lights and shifting sand —
Black way and rough and long —
Lost men and like to fail —
This much is ours:

Sometimes to strike a trail,
Sometimes to hear a song,
Sometimes to seize a hand,
I even yours.

Go with me till the sun
Mine be and yours,
Star and companion,
Ours, even ours.

The Rose

How praise the rose! Let praise go by:
Let us not praise where praising were
To underpraise; we may come nigh,
Withholding praise, to praising her.

Quarter-Day

DEATH asked: the debtor bit his lip
And offered something on account;
Death smiled and took a closer grip:
The debtor paid the full amount.

The Night

FOND Muse, surrender, weary as thou art,
　　To sleep at last; a meadow's breadth from thee,
In yon dim copse and still, a sister heart
　　Hath respite from its old sweet agony.

The wall of night is up; around, across,
　　Above nor sound nor sense of day remains;
Comes only now the fitful drive and toss
　　Of moths upon the yellow window-panes.

An Erring Muse

OUT! Wretched Rhyme, and none of my begetting!
    Quit! Go thy ways; I say I'll none of thee!
Fie on thee, Muse, that thou shouldst go coquetting
    With every losel that would sport with me.

Now am I one whom Fate hath countered slyly;
    In me behold a bard dispirited —
Joined with a Muse whom Mischance, jesting dryly,
    To spite my fame hath sued and brought to bed.

Where wert thou, Metre, when the churl espied her,
    And planned to mar the lustre of my song?
Wherefore was thy protection then denied her,
    To her undoing and my lyric wrong?

Go to! I will to Prose and win his favour.
    Too soon my lyric wine is at the lee;
Too soon my lyric salt hath lost its savour;
    I will to Prose and pray him succour me.

Nay, go! I'm stone: I say I'll not resume her.
    Her mention adds new venom to my smart!
Ay, get her hence! let pies and crows unplume her,
    And blank annihilation end her part!

One moment still, let me upbraid her roundly!
    Was never bard so villainously vexed
And put about by trollop Muse, but soundly
    I will repay who hath me thus perplexed.

Thou cart-tail queen! Go, blandish with thine ogles
    The bloodless breast of midnight's baleful king;
From his embrace let riving imps and bogles,
    Ghast moonlight jinn, and morrow-madness spring.

Lost dam of Mischief! Dost thou hope to melt me
   With tears less salt than those whose scalding brine
Clings round the thrust thy evil gaming dealt me,
   To smart its depth while mortal years are mine?

She weeps, she only weeps, nor heeds nor hears me.
   At every turn I face ill fortune's prong,
Yet know not whether most her weeping tears me,
   Or I am torn with anger at my wrong.

Ay me! I would not mete her fault too shrewdly,
   Nor nag her to an ecstasy of shame;
Whom once I loved I would not drive too rudely
   To wail in exile her lost lyric name.

Nay, how shall I, least worthy son of Adam,
   Glad heir to half the sins he left entail,
Deliver judgment on this erring madam,
   Compel her to a convent and the veil?

Now 'shrew me that would send a woman weeping,
   What was the work this pother's all about?
It seems some mischance found my metre sleeping,
   Whose place it was to keep such rascals out.

Well then? Well then, what doth the scurvy varlet
   But whisk my lady off without a word.
And she? And she, she says, went crimson scarlet
   And screamed like anything, but no one heard.

And then? And then, of course, the raff besought her
   With 'pretty' this and 'pretty' that — in brief,
To such a pass this woundy mischief brought her,
   That she hath borne a brat beyond belief.

Well there, maybe I've split a straw too finely,
  Too bitter mixed an erring Muse's cup;
I must look on such matters more benignly. . . .
  Ay, I'll entreat a kiss and make it up.

Two eyes of tears! What, human, can withstand 'em,
  Ten thousand angers trumpeting their force?
Two eyes of tears will presently disband 'em,
  And list 'em into armies of remorse.

Then come, sweet Muse, no longer nurse thy sorrow;
  I'll father this and any rhyme of thine;
Forget as I forgive, and I to-morrow
  Will advertise the world the babe is mine.

An Elegy upon a Poem Ruined by a Clumsy Metre

GAZE on thy deed, damned Metre, and be dumb!
　Lies dead the Joy that sought in thy embrace
A hostelry, and found, alas! a tomb:
　Look, and with penitential tears efface

From memory the scarlet of thy sin.
　Yet ere erasure sun thy soul again,
Brook my brief lamentation; let me win
　For that last effluence of my fevered brain

A niche in Fame's high temple. . . . Jewel rare
　As ever yet from that dim pit and deep,
Man's mind, was dug: sweet flower and frail as fair,
　Too early wakened from a wintry sleep —

For thee I mourn and pitch a peevish key!
　Spring from thy wat'ry pillow, Truth, and hear;
Come, sisters twain, thou clear-eyed Sanity
　And stern-browed Sense, come lend a patient ear.

Oft with Imagination I have bored
　And tunnelled like a mole the sacred soil
Of Poesy; and with her I have soared
　Above the clouds to spy among and spoil

The furthest fields of Heaven; at her command
　I've walked below the sea and cut my way
Through mucous wrecks that strew the stretchèd sand
　'Twixt western Ind and impotent Cathay;

And in her sight, beneath an English sky,
　I've shared his dreams who on the Asian plain
Left crook and shears and rode to empery,
　And half a world bowed under Tamerlane.

Old Druids on the downs have watched with me
    For revelation from a silent star,
And I, as even they, have bent a knee
    To Caturix, and sung with them to war.

I've read the books : stained record of Man hurled
    Against himself; thus taught each ruined page —
From birth to adolescence spun the world
    Through tides of woe, and will to wrinkled age.

Save that drear lore small profit there was mine;
    Yet this : who breaks the idols of Man's past,
To build anew for men a later shrine,
    But builds to be his own iconoclast.

Ev'n in the dim recess of my own mind
    I've dared to look; held inquisition there,
Strange riddles solved and mysteries divined,
    Nigh laid the secret of my being bare;

Seen impulse in the seed whose sudden flower
    Too often blows to hide a barbèd stem;
Seen Pleasure, surfeit with her own sweet dower,
    Fade to a spectre with a diadem.

There in the seventh cellar of my soul
    I've crushed the stone where Malice tipped her spears;
And raked the dust of Anger's burnt-out coal,
    And watched with awe the genesis of tears.

And this fair thing I've seen : Hope, lightning bright,
    But not inconstant like the sword of Heaven,
And smiling still in her own dear despite
    When Desperation through my soul has driven.

But not for me Imagination throve
　　From song-born seed new ecstasy so wild,
Nor woke lost captain's battle shouts and wove
　　Wild dream so new as wert thou, her dead Child.

Nor ever to Imagination's wand
　　Came aught so rare from land or sky or sea,
Nor aught so shy or bright or strange I scanned
　　When Introspection bared my depths to me;

Nor in the stainèd books I found displayed,
　　Though angels wept there, tear so pure; nor I,
From wrecked beliefs whose altars long withstayed
　　Truth's certain tide, beheld, that might not die,

One pale flame kindle beautiful as wert
　　Thou, unblown Flower and fadeless : lo! beneath
These lilac boughs, in warm grass pansy-girt,
　　I hide thy urn and leave this rhymèd wreath.

The Vanity of Human Ambition and Big Behaviour

O NOW all ye whom Arrogance brought low,
  Whom Folly or Illusion's Judas-kiss
Entangled in a labyrinth of woe —
  Children of Dream and heirs of Nemesis —

Awake, arise, and let your deeds be told;
  Come forth and in Dissuasion's service win
The little not denied your deeds of old:
  Fame's door is wide, ye need but enter in.

Behold as thick as gnats at evenglow
  They come a jaunty herohood, agog
To turn this work — if I may put it so —
  Into a lyric Dic. of Nat. Biog.

A pushing fellow, seeking note and fame,
  Went out to break a lance with Xiphias;
Archbishop Willson says our hero's name
  Was Coe. The learned prelate, if he, as

One likes to think, spoke not without the book
  Before he disallowed such names as Lee,
Burdette and Gray, and Parkinson and Hook,
  And Mackintosh and Dixon and McGee,[1]

As having claims too shadowy and thin
  For cold consideration in the case,
Might anyway have said where Coe's came in:
  Occasion finds odd logic in his Grace.[2]

But Parkinson, Coe, Dixon, or Burdette,
  Lee, Mackintosh, or Hook, McGee or Gray,

[1] *Life and Letters*, edited by Llewellen Lane. Also see *Side-saddle and Steamboat in South Europe*, by Lady Grahame-Price.
[2] As witness his peculiar views on the Ruyan Monarchy, *Life and Letters*, chap. xxiii.

He died B.C., to Pompeii's regret;
  The good Archbishop, too, has passed away.

The tale, then, it is mine to tell will show
  To what unseemly shift a bard is pressed,
Who, doubting not the evidence for Coe,
  Would neither in discredit hold the rest.

Did Mackintosh know fear? The slender bill
  Wherewith he armed to turn the other's blade,
And swift thereafter pink him in the gill,
  Was tough and keen. Burdette was not afraid.

Hook eyed the fish. The argent orb of night
  With tender longing wan looked on the sea,
And flung a wreath of kisses to the white
  Young wanton waves. The monster eyed McGee.

Gray stood his ground. The supersensuous air
  Toyed sadly with the shimmering strands of spray
That, like a languid naiad's tangled hair,
  Shone opalescent. Lee now looked away.

For Parkinson was bored. The lucent wave
  With rhythmic lassitude fell to and fro
O'er many a spongy lawn and haunted cave
  Of dim crustacea. Dixon turned to go.

Then time was called; above Night's widening plume
  With numerous glimmering stars was gemmed about,
Whose pale effulgence fell to re-illume
  The sun-lorn waste, and Coe was counted out.

Not with the noise and blare of sounded brass
  And common hum that marks a prince returned,
But like the gent who comes about the gas,
  Unasked, unblest, unkissed, and unconcerned,

48

Truth comes to Man (who rarely questions whence
　　Or why, if come she must, she comes so late)
And takes the sum of his incompetence,
　　And drops a tract and leaves him to his fate.

One sore chagrined with envy of the Cid,
　　Came out of Crim by way of the Levant,
And sailed to Spain and settled in Madrid,
　　And looked about and wagered a byzant

That he would snare, disarm, and bring to land
　　The stoutest cuttle in the Spanish Main,
And jumped off Gib. and snared a cuttle, and
　　Came never more upon the coast of Spain.

Not Policy, slow tracing like a worm,
　　Circuitous and dim through sunless ways,
To crown a painful, calculated term
　　With high achievement and a people's praise,

But Impulse, blind, inconsequent, and vain,
　　Called on the joyless mameluke, Githar —
Whom John of Teflis lost to Smandercane
　　When last he met the Usbec prince in war —

To pelt his uncle Selim with the soap
　　What time the elder took his morning tub.
Did Uncle Selim wanly smile and hope
　　That time would yet teach manners to the cub?

Or did he rise as, reader, thou hadst done,
　　And as in honour he was bound to do,
And talk it over with his sister's son?
　　These knew and wept the course he took, these knew:

Melodious bulbuls in the almond trees,
  The flaming carp that lit the palace pond,
The doe-led fawns in forest fastnesses
  That twisted many a tangled mile beyond;

And on the windy hills the antelopes,
  And gibbering bats in scented lemon groves,
And eagles screaming at the mountain tops,
  And in the gloomy cedars cushat doves;

And in the hot blue sky the wand'ring crane,
  And in the hot blue sky the circling kite,
And on the hot, eye-baffling desert plain,
  Dry, gliding things of fell or futile spite;

And in the folded leaf the folded worm,
  And dreaming in the bark the chrysalis,
And in the soaring, wind-borne seed the germ
  Of jungles yet to know their genesis;

And at the lonely well mid Ira's heat,
  In tent or dhow or bagnio or bazar,
At silent tomb or in the swarming street,
  From Trebizonde and Kars to Bussarah,

From Antioch to Tartar Samarkand,
  Boor, bassa, bedouin, infidel, and Turk:
These knew and wept Githar's mad folly, and
  These knew what supervened upon his work.

No tyrant drunk with pride and armed with power,
  His throne a shambles and his music war,
No hero hot and ripened to the hour,
  And for its quick salvation singular,

Was Jil the Giaur, a lad of Ascalon,
　Whose humour crost the toothèd thing of Nile:
His tibia turned up, and long time won
　From women tears, from men a mirthless smile.

At Susa by the Midland Sea, one Tegg,
　A potboy and reputed for a quiz,
No reptiles handy, pulled the pieman's leg;
　The boy, however, got away with his.

The Bagdad Pipe-rolls tell how one, a beau,
　Kicked McHaroun, the barber, for a joke,
How caution ruled the canny figaro,
　And what Mac done to pay the fancy bloke.

Now from the gloom that wraps two nameless stones,
　The shades of . . . and . . . invite my pen
To trace their faulty day, and from their bones
　Pick wisdom in the name of living men.

Their earthly habitat was Bagdad town,
　And, as coevals of the barber Mac,
Were subjects of that prince who owed his crown
　To brother Achmet sleeping on his back.

With soundy argument at dawn they met,
　And saw the sun go down the Occident
(Ay me! where late another sun had set
　For Avon stream) with soundy argument.

They bragged in terms of angle, hound, and lure,
　Of family, of friend, of dice and ball,
Of virtue, vice, and love, and literature,
　And grew, by easy stages, personal.

'Thou cringing turnspit! with thy kin debate!
  Peace, ere some mastiff tire of thee and thrust,
With too much honour for thy mean estate,
  A peevish paw and merge thee with the dust!'

'Nay, upstart bantam, strut with them thy size;
  Crow back thy kidneys' with an equal note;
Contend with such as, beating thee, would prize
  The lowly glory of thy silenced throat!'

'Be dumb, glib pyot, lest thy noise offend
  The eyried falcon's sense till, wearied, he
Incline his wing thy way and condescend
  To stoop and strike and, striking, cancel thee!'

They scowled, lip-weary; stars came over new;
  The stars looked on them and a moonbeam fell;
The moonbeam lit them as they went unto
  An antique chamber looking on the Mall.

And there for aye they laid their tongues to rest,
  And took them staves and locked the attic door,
And drew the window-blind, and never guessed
  The frail condition of the attic floor.

So stood these lads to arms, all unaware
  What fiends and angels pitied them or mocked,
What fiends and angels trod the attic stair,
  And entered by the door on mortals locked.

Thus, masking in the winter face of Truth,
  Came Disillusion, dreary ghost, and sped
A fletchèd arrow barbed with Reason's tooth —
  That instant Hope fell bleeding and lay dead.

Came Hate, sure signet still of serpent power
   In human hearts, and with obscene excess
Joyed in the clasp of Scorn; the pride and flower
   And pink of devildom came there to press

Their sovereign's loathly suit with added spite
   For that dread Hour ere yet the first slow beat
Of young Time's pulse responded to the flight
   Of years; came thither, too, on wandering feet

Whom men name Chance, nor seemed he well to know
   What brought him to that place, what faithful star
Or faithless urged his stay, yet did he throw
   Among his peers assembled wide and far —

If I may use the term when all were met
   Beneath a ceiling twelve feet by fifteen —
No little consternation, so he set
   A good example, and no more was seen.

Now Expectation waited in the air,
   And ten-tongued Rumour from her leash ran free —
A mouthy brach; came from her fetid lair
   The bat-eyed harridan old Prophecy,

Her ashen locks wild strewn about her brow;
   And Licence came, sweet Liberty's rude twin;
Mute over all hung heedless Fate, and now
   The palsied despot Crisis shuffled in.

Here leave the lads: I would not were detailed
   Their story further; only would I tell
That midnight's gilt elaboration paled
   Above a silent attic on the Mall. . . .

The Caliph Ali went to Ispahan
  And backed a mule there in a steeplechase;
His fancy won, and then the bookie ran;
  The punter lost a pony on the race.

Likewise the Cypriot El Ezra, he
  Who took a tester to a ducatoon
About the colt by Nix-Mnemosyne
  To win the Sherbet Stakes at Scandaroon,

What fun was his? Who so will stake his lot,
  Impelled thereto by nescience or whim,
Cupidity or innocence or not,
  On Chance's colours, let men pray for him.

Yet may he sit serene and well content,
  When others nose the future for his hurt,
Who, beautiful and wise and prescient,
  Shall gamble all he hath upon a cert.

Ah, little thought King Cheops long ago —
  Yet wherefore, to what end, why deeper drink
At brackish wells and fountains of old woe!
  What matters now what Cheops didn't think!

What matters now what siren song beguiled
  The steps of Mna, most loved of Andæ's sons,
Or that in Coac's sun-charged desert wild
  He wrote repentance with his whited bones!

Nay, cease; Dissuasion cannot surely ask
  A shrewder schedule of Oblivion's gains;
O cease! my Muse is weary of her task,
  And would on other themes expend her pains.

Dulcina, A Bull-Terrier

Dulcina was, then suns rebelled
  And trod th' eternal word;
To every ball its limits held,
  The universe was stirred.

World embryons, in chaos rolled,
  Knew system at her cry,
And hoary planets ages cold
  Policed anew the sky.

Suns came and sun's star's satellites
  To sing Dulcina's power,
And myriad moons left myriad nights
  To keep a pagan hour.

In rebel red extravagance
  The flaming legions came;
In her transplendent brilliance
  They paled to candle flame,

And praised above all dams her dam,
  And gave her sire reward,
And hailed me blest o'er all who am
  Her bondsman and her bard;

Who sees in her all things glassed fair,
  And Paradise would fly,
That wanting her were angel-bare
  And drear felicity.

The Great Auk's Ghost

THE Great Auk's ghost rose on one leg,
    Sighed thrice and three times winkt,
And turned and poached a phantom egg,
    And muttered, 'I'm extinct.'

The Final Dodo

THE final Dodo gathered wool
  Upon a mountain side;
His energy was wonderful,
  And finally he died.

Farewell

Go, little book; fear not thy fate;
Though men deride and rail
And pass thee by, yet Truth is great,
By Jove! and will prevail.

To My Muse

O MELIC Muse, whose constant love
    Sustained my timorous reed;
Darned threadbare Fancy's vest, or wove
    New garments to her need;

Cheered Metre when his heart was down,
    Or gently plied the spur,
And brought us all to Finis Town
    To seek a Publisher:

Go not! Brave heart, and gay as true,
    Till Time ebb out stay by
To teach my straw, then let us two
    Pipe down Eternity.

The Gipsy Girl

'COME, try your skill, kind gentlemen,
A penny for three tries!'
Some threw and lost, some threw and won
A ten-a-penny prize.

She was a tawny gipsy girl,
A girl of twenty years,
I liked her for the lumps of gold
That jingled from her ears;

I liked the flaring yellow scarf
Bound loose about her throat,
I liked her showy purple gown
And flashy velvet coat.

A man came up, too loose of tongue,
And said no good to her;
She did not blush as Saxons do,
Or turn upon the cur;

She fawned and whined 'Sweet gentleman,
A penny for three tries!'
— But oh, the den of wild things in
The darkness of her eyes!

A Song

WITH Love among the haycocks
We played at hide and seek;

He shut his eyes and counted —
We hid among the hay —
Then he a haycock mounted,
And spied us where we lay;

And O! the merry laughter
Across the hayfield after!

Time, you Old Gipsy Man

TIME, you old gipsy man,
  Will you not stay,
Put up your caravan
  Just for one day?

All things I'll give you
Will you be my guest,
Bells for your jennet
Of silver the best,
Goldsmiths shall beat you
A great golden ring,
Peacocks shall bow to you,
Little boys sing,
Oh, and sweet girls will
Festoon you with may,
Time, you old gipsy,
Why hasten away?

Last week in Babylon,
Last night in Rome,
Morning, and in the crush
Under Paul's dome;
Under Paul's dial
You tighten your rein —
Only a moment,
And off once again;
Off to some city
Now blind in the womb,
Off to another
Ere that's in the tomb.

Time, you old gipsy man,
  Will you not stay,
Put up your caravan
  Just for one day?

Ghoul Care

SOUR fiend, go home and tell the Pit
For once you met your master, —
A man who carried in his soul
Three charms against disaster,
The Devil and disaster.

Away, away, and tell the tale
And start your whelps a-whining,
Say 'In the greenwood of his soul
A lizard's eye was shining,
A little eye kept shining.'

Away, away, and salve your sores,
And set your hags a-groaning,
Say 'In the greenwood of his soul
A drowsy bee was droning,
A dreamy bee was droning.'

Prodigious Bat! Go start the walls
Of Hell with horror ringing,
Say 'In the greenwood of his soul
There was a goldfinch singing,
A pretty goldfinch singing.'

And then come back, come, if you please,
A fiercer ghoul and ghaster,
With all the glooms and smuts of Hell
Behind you, I'm your master!
You know I'm still your master.

Eve

EVE, with her basket, was
Deep in the bells and grass,
Wading in bells and grass
Up to her knees,
Picking a dish of sweet
Berries and plums to eat,
Down in the bells and grass
Under the trees.

Mute as a mouse in a
Corner the cobra lay,
Curled round a bough of the
Cinnamon tall. . . .
Now to get even and
Humble proud Heaven and
Now was the moment or
Never at all.

'Eva!' Each syllable
Light as a flower fell,
'Eva!' he whispered the
Wondering maid,
Soft as a bubble sung
Out of a linnet's lung,
Soft and most silverly
'Eva!' he said.

Picture that orchard sprite,
Eve, with her body white,
Supple and smooth to her
Slim finger tips,
Wondering, listening,
Listening, wondering,
Eve with a berry
Half-way to her lips.

Oh had our simple Eve
Seen through the make-believe!
Had she but known the
Pretender he was!
Out of the boughs he came,
Whispering still her name,
Tumbling in twenty rings
Into the grass.

Here was the strangest pair
In the world anywhere,
Eve in the bells and grass
Kneeling, and he
Telling his story low. . . .
Singing birds saw them go
Down the dark path to
The Blasphemous Tree.

Oh what a clatter when
Titmouse and Jenny Wren
Saw him successful and
Taking his leave!
How the birds rated him,
How they all hated him!
How they all pitied
Poor motherless Eve!

Picture her crying
Outside in the lane,
Eve, with no dish of sweet
Berries and plums to eat,
Haunting the gate of the
Orchard in vain. . . .
Picture the lewd delight
Under the hill to-night —
'Eva!' the toast goes round,
'Eva!' again.

The Song of Honour

I CLIMBED a hill as light fell short,
And rooks came home in scramble sort,
And filled the trees and flapped and fought
And sang themselves to sleep;
An owl from nowhere with no sound
Swung by and soon was nowhere found,
I heard him calling half-way round,
Holloing loud and deep;
A pair of stars, faint pins of light,
Then many a star, sailed into sight,
And all the stars, the flower of night,
Were round me at a leap;
To tell how still the valleys lay
I heard a watchdog miles away,
And bells of distant sheep.

I heard no more of bird or bell,
The mastiff in a slumber fell,
I stared into the sky,
As wondering men have always done
Since beauty and the stars were one,
Though none so hard as I.

It seemed, so still the valleys were,
As if the whole world knelt at prayer,
Save me and me alone;
So pure and wide that silence was
I feared to bend a blade of grass,
And there I stood like stone.

66

There, sharp and sudden, there I heard —
Ah! some wild lovesick singing bird
Woke singing in the trees?
The nightingale and babble-wren
Were in the English greenwood then,
And you heard one of these?

The babble-wren and nightingale
Sang in the Abyssinian vale
That season of the year!
Yet, true enough, I heard them plain,
I heard them both again, again,
As sharp and sweet and clear
As if the Abyssinian tree
Had thrust a bough across the sea,
Had thrust a bough across to me
With music for my ear!

I heard them both, and oh! I heard
The song of every singing bird
That sings beneath the sky,
And with the song of lark and wren
The song of mountains, moths and men
And seas and rainbows vie!

I heard the universal choir,
The Sons of Light exalt their Sire
With universal song,
Earth's lowliest and loudest notes,
Her million times ten million throats
Exalt Him loud and long,
And lips and lungs and tongues of Grace
From every part and every place
Within the shining of His face,
The universal throng.

I heard the hymn of being sound
From every well of honour found
In human sense and soul:
The song of poets when they write
The testament of Beautysprite
Upon a flying scroll,
The song of painters when they take
A burning brush for Beauty's sake
And limn her features whole —

The song of men divinely wise
Who look and see in starry skies
Not stars so much as robins' eyes,
And when these pale away
Hear flocks of shiny pleiades
Among the plums and apple trees
Sing in the summer day —

The song of all both high and low
To some blest vision true,
The song of beggars when they throw
The crust of pity all men owe
To hungry sparrows in the snow,
Old beggars hungry too —
The song of kings of kingdoms when
They rise above their fortune Men,
And crown themselves anew —

The song of courage, heart and will
And gladness in a fight,
Of men who face a hopeless hill
With sparking and delight,
The bells and bells of song that ring
Round banners of a cause or king
From armies bleeding white —

The song of sailors every one
When monstrous tide and tempest run
At ships like bulls at red,
When stately ships are twirled and spun
Like whipping-tops and help there's none
And mighty ships ten thousand ton
Go down like lumps of lead —

And song of fighters stern as they
At odds with fortune night and day,
Crammed up in cities grim and gray
As thick as bees in hives,
Hosannas of a lowly throng
Who sing unconscious of their song,
Whose lips are in their lives —

And song of some at holy war
With spells and ghouls more dread by far
Than deadly seas and cities are
Or hordes of quarrelling kings —
The song of fighters great and small,
The song of pretty fighters all
And high heroic things —

The song of lovers — who knows how
Twitched up from place and time
Upon a sigh, a blush, a vow,
A curve or hue of cheek or brow,
Borne up and off from here and now
Into the void sublime!

And crying loves and passions still
In every key from soft to shrill
And numbers never done,
Dog-loyalties to faith and friend,
And loves like Ruth's of old no end,
And intermission none —

And burst on burst for beauty and
For numbers not behind,
From men whose love of motherland
Is like a dog's for one dear hand,
Sole, selfless, boundless, blind —
And song of some with hearts beside
For men and sorrows far and wide,
Who watch the world with pity and pride
And warm to all mankind —

And endless joyous music rise
From children at their play,
And endless soaring lullabies
From happy, happy mothers' eyes,
And answering crows and baby-cries,
How many who shall say!
And many a song as wondrous well
With pangs and sweets intolerable
From lonely hearths too gray to tell,
God knows how utter gray!
And song from many a house of care
When pain has forced a footing there
And there's a Darkness on the stair
Will not be turned away —

And song — that song whose singers come
With old kind tales of pity from
The Great Compassion's lips,
That make the bells of Heaven to peal
Round pillows frosty with the feel
Of Death's cold finger tips —

The song of men all sorts and kinds,
As many tempers, moods and minds
As leaves are on a tree,
As many faiths and castes and creeds,
As many human bloods and breeds
As in the world may be;

The song of each and all who gaze
On Beauty in her naked blaze,
Or see her dimly in a haze,
Or get her light in fitful rays
And tiniest needles even,
The song of all not wholly dark,
Not wholly sunk in stupor stark
Too deep for groping Heaven —

And alleluias sweet and clear
And wild with beauty men mishear,
From choirs of song as near and dear
To Paradise as they,
The everlasting pipe and flute
Of wind and sea and bird and brute,
And lips deaf men imagine mute
In wood and stone and clay:

The music of a lion strong
That shakes a hill a whole night long,
A hill as loud as he,
The twitter of a mouse among
Melodious greenery,
The ruby's and the rainbow's song,
The nightingale's — all three,
The song of life that wells and flows
From every leopard, lark and rose
And everything that gleams or goes
Lack-lustre in the sea.

I heard it all, each, every note
Of every lung and tongue and throat,
Ay, every rhythm and rhyme
Of everything that lives and loves
And upward, ever upward moves
From lowly to sublime!
Earth's multitudinous Sons of Light,
I heard them lift their lyric might
With each and every chanting sprite
That lit the sky that wondrous night
As far as eye could climb!

I heard it all, I heard the whole
Harmonious hymn of being roll
Up through the chapel of my soul
And at the altar die,
And in the awful quiet then
Myself I heard, Amen, Amen,
Amen I heard me cry!
I heard it all and then although
I caught my flying senses, Oh,
A dizzy man was I!
I stood and stared; the sky was lit,
The sky was stars all over it,
I stood, I knew not why,
Without a wish, without a will,
I stood upon that silent hill
And stared into the sky until
My eyes were blind with stars and still
I stared into the sky.

The Mystery

He came and took me by the hand
   Up to a red rose tree,
He kept His meaning to Himself
   But gave a rose to me.

I did not pray Him to lay bare
   The mystery to me,
Enough the rose was Heaven to smell,
   And His own face to see.

Stupidity Street

I saw with open eyes
Singing birds sweet
Sold in the shops
For the people to eat,
Sold in the shops of
Stupidity Street.

I saw in vision
The worm in the wheat,
And in the shops nothing
For people to eat;
Nothing for sale in
Stupidity Street.

The Bells of Heaven

'Twould ring the bells of Heaven
The wildest peal for years,
If Parson lost his senses
And people came to theirs,
And he and they together
Knelt down with angry prayers
For tamed and shabby tigers
And dancing dogs and bears,
And wretched, blind pit ponies,
And little hunted hares.

The Journeyman

NOT baser than his own homekeeping kind
Whose journeyman he is —
Blind sons and breastless daughters of the blind
Whose darkness pardons his, —
About the world, while all the world approves,
The pimp of Fashion steals,
With all the angels mourning their dead loves
Behind his bloody heels.

It may be late when Nature cries Enough!
As one day cry she will,
And man may have the wit to put her off
With shifts a season still;
But man may find the pinch importunate
And fall to blaming men —
Blind sires and breastless mothers of his fate,
It may be late and may be very late,
Too late for blaming then.

The Bull

SEE an old unhappy bull,
Sick in soul and body both,
Slouching in the undergrowth
Of the forest beautiful,
Banished from the herd he led,
Bulls and cows a thousand head.

Cranes and gaudy parrots go
Up and down the burning sky;
Tree-top cats purr drowsily
In the dim-day green below;
And troops of monkeys, nutting, some,
All disputing, go and come;

And things abominable sit
Picking offal buck or swine,
On the mess and over it
Burnished flies and beetles shine,
And spiders big as bladders lie
Under hemlocks ten foot high;

And a dotted serpent curled
Round and round and round a tree,
Yellowing its greenery,
Keeps a watch on all the world,
All the world and this old bull
In the forest beautiful.

Bravely by his fall he came:
One he led, a bull of blood
Newly come to lustihood,
Fought and put his prince to shame,
Snuffed and pawed the prostrate head
Tameless even while it bled.

There they left him, every one,
Left him there without a lick,
Left him for the birds to pick,
Left him there for carrion,
Vilely from their bosom cast
Wisdom, worth and love at last.

When the lion left his lair
And roared his beauty through the hills,
And the vultures pecked their quills
And flew into the middle air,
Then this prince no more to reign
Came to life and lived again.

He snuffed the herd in far retreat,
He saw the blood upon the ground,
And snuffed the burning airs around
Still with beevish odours sweet,
While the blood ran down his head
And his mouth ran slaver red.

Pity him, this fallen chief,
All his splendour, all his strength,
All his body's breadth and length
Dwindled down with shame and grief,
Half the bull he was before,
Bones and leather, nothing more.

See him standing dewlap-deep
In the rushes at the lake,
Surly, stupid, half asleep,
Waiting for his heart to break
And the birds to join the flies
Feasting at his bloodshot eyes;

Standing with his head hung down
In a stupor, dreaming things:
Green savannas, jungles brown,
Battlefields and bellowings,
Bulls undone and lions dead
And vultures flapping overhead.

Dreaming things: of days he spent
With his mother gaunt and lean
In the valley warm and green,
Full of baby wonderment,
Blinking out of silly eyes
At a hundred mysteries;

Dreaming over once again
How he wandered with a throng
Of bulls and cows a thousand strong,
Wandered on from plain to plain,
Up the hill and down the dale,
Always at his mother's tail;

How he lagged behind the herd,
Lagged and tottered, weak of limb,
And she turned and ran to him
Blaring at the loathly bird
Stationed always in the skies,
Waiting for the flesh that dies.

Dreaming maybe of a day
When her drained and drying paps
Turned him to the sweets and saps,
Richer fountains by the way,
And she left the bull she bore
And he looked to her no more;

79

And his little frame grew stout,
And his little legs grew strong,
And the way was not so long;
And his little horns came out,
And he played at butting trees
And boulder-stones and tortoises,

Joined a game of knobby skulls
With the youngsters of his year,
All the other little bulls,
Learning both to bruise and bear,
Learning how to stand a shock
Like a little bull of rock.

Dreaming of a day less dim,
Dreaming of a time less far,
When the faint but certain star
Of destiny burned clear for him,
And a fierce and wild unrest
Broke the quiet of his breast,

And the gristles of his youth
Hardened in his comely pow,
And he came to fighting growth,
Beat his bull and won his cow,
And flew his tail and trampled off
Past the tallest, vain enough,

And curved about in splendour full
And curved again and snuffed the airs
As who should say Come out who dares!
And all beheld a bull, a Bull,
And knew that here was surely one
That backed for no bull, fearing none.

And the leader of the herd
Looked and saw, and beat the ground,
And shook the forest with his sound,
Bellowed at the loathly bird
Stationed always in the skies,
Waiting for the flesh that dies.

Dreaming, this old bull forlorn,
Surely dreaming of the hour
When he came to sultan power,
And they owned him master-horn,
Chiefest bull of all among
Bulls and cows a thousand strong;

And in all the tramping herd
Not a bull that barred his way,
Not a cow that said him nay,
Not a bull or cow that erred
In the furnace of his look
Dared a second, worse rebuke;

Not in all the forest wide,
Jungle, thicket, pasture, fen,
Not another dared him then,
Dared him and again defied;
Not a sovereign buck or boar
Came a second time for more;

Not a serpent that survived
Once the terrors of his hoof
Risked a second time reproof,
Came a second time and lived,
Not a serpent in its skin
Came again for discipline;

Not a leopard bright as flame,
Flashing fingerhooks of steel
That a wooden tree might feel,
Met his fury once and came
For a second reprimand,
Not a leopard in the land;

Not a lion of them all,
Not a lion of the hills,
Hero of a thousand kills,
Dared a second fight and fall,
Dared that ram terrific twice,
Paid a second time the price. . . .

Pity him, this dupe of dream,
Leader of the herd again
Only in his daft old brain,
Once again the bull supreme
And bull enough to bear the part
Only in his tameless heart.

Pity him that he must wake;
Even now the swarm of flies
Blackening his bloodshot eyes
Bursts and blusters round the lake,
Scattered from the feast half-fed,
By great shadows overhead.

And the dreamer turns away
From his visionary herds
And his splendid yesterday,
Turns to meet the loathly birds
Flocking round him from the skies,
Waiting for the flesh that dies.

Playmates

It's sixty years ago, the people say:
Two village children, neighbours born and bred,
One morning played beneath a rotten tree
That came down crash and caught them as they fled;
And one was killed and one was left unhurt
Except for certain fancies in his head.

And though it's all so very long ago
He's never left the wood a single day;
I've often met him peeping through the leaves
And chuckling to himself, an old man gray;

And once he started in his cracked old voice:
'We're playing I'm a merchant lost his way,
She's robbers in the wood behind yon tree,
The minute we grow up too big to play—'

The House Across the Way

THE leaves looked in at the window
Of the house across the way,
At a man that had sinned like you and me
And all poor human clay.

He muttered: 'In a gambol
I took my soul astray,
But to-morrow I'll drag it back from danger,
In the morning, come what may;
For no man knows what season
He shall go his ghostly way.'
And his face fell down upon the table,
And where it fell it lay.

And the wind blew under the carpet
And it said, or it seemed to say:
'Truly, all men must go a-ghosting
And no man knows his day.'
And the leaves stared in at the window
Like the people at a play.

The Beggar

HE begged and shuffled on;
Sometimes he stopped to throw
A bit and benison
To sparrows in the snow,
And clap a frozen ear
And curse the bitter cold.
God send the good man cheer
And quittal hundredfold.

Babylon

I f you could bring her glories back!
You gentle sirs who sift the dust
And burrow in the mould and must
Of Babylon for bric-à-brac;
Who catalogue and pigeon-hole
The faded splendours of her soul
And put her greatness under glass —
If you could bring her past to pass!

If you could bring her dead to life!
The soldier lad; the market wife;
Madam buying fowls from her;
Tip, the butcher's bandy cur;
Workmen carting bricks and clay;
Babel passing to and fro
On the business of a day
Gone three thousand years ago ——

That you cannot; then be done,
Put the goblet down again,
Let the broken arch remain,
Leave the dead men's dust alone ——

Is it nothing how she lies,
This old mother of you all,
You great cities proud and tall
Towering to a hundred skies
Round a world she never knew,
Is it nothing, this, to you?
Must the ghoulish work go on
Till her very floors are gone?
While there's still a brick to save
Drive these people from her grave.

The Jewish seer when he cried
Woe to Babel's lust and pride
Saw the foxes at her gates;
Once again the wild thing waits.
Then leave her in her last decay
A house of owls, a foxes' den;
The desert that till yesterday
Hid her from the eyes of men
In its proper time and way
Will take her to itself again.

The Moor

THE world's gone forward to its latest fair
And dropt an old man done with by the way,
To sit alone among the bats and stare
At miles and miles and miles of moorland bare
Lit only with last shreds of dying day.

Not all the world, not all the world's gone by:
Old man, you're like to meet one traveller still,
A journeyman well kenned for courtesy
To all that walk at odds with life and limb;
If this be he now riding up the hill
Maybe he'll stop and take you up with him. . . .

'But thou art Death?' 'Of Heavenly Seraphim
None else to seek thee out and bid thee come.'
'I only care that thou art come from Him,
Unbody me — I'm tired — and get me home.'

February

A FEW tossed thrushes save
That carolled less than cried
Against the dying rave
And moan that never died,
No bird sang then; no thorn,
No tree was green beside
Them only never shorn —
The few by all the winds
And chill mutations born
Of Winter's many minds
Abused and whipt in vain —
Swarth yew and ivy kinds
And iron breeds germane.

The Late, Last Rook

THE old gilt vane and spire receive
The last beam eastward striking;
The first shy bat to peep at eve
Has found her to his liking.
The western heaven is dull and gray,
The last red glow has followed day.

The late, last rook is housed and will
With cronies lie till morrow;
If there's a rook loquacious still
In dream he hunts a furrow,
And flaps behind a spectre team,
Or ghostly scarecrows walk his dream.

The Birdcatcher

WHEN flighting time is on I go
With clap-net and decoy,
A-fowling after goldfinches
And other birds of joy;

I lurk among the thickets of
The Heart where they are bred,
And catch the twittering beauties as
They fly into my Head.

The Royal Mails

For all its flowers and trailing bowers,
Its singing birds and streams,
This valley's not the blissful spot.
The paradise, it seems.

I don't forget a man I met
Beneath this very tree, —
The cooing of that cushat dove
Brings back his face to me, —
The merest lad, a sullen, sad,
Unhappy soul with eyes half mad,
Most sorrowful to see.

I asked him who he was, and what;
'Twas his affair, he answered, that,
And had no more to say;
'Twas all I'd feared, the tale I heard,
When he at last gave way.

I've not forgot the look he shot
Me through and through with then;
'What loathly land is this!' he cried,
And cursed it for a countryside
Where devils masque as men.

I thought at first his brain was burst,
So senselessly he cried and cursed
And spat with rage and hate;
He writhed to hear the glossy dove
In song among the boughs above
Beside its gentle mate.

His fury passed away at last,
And when his reason came
He told me he was city bred,
A page about the Court, he said,
And coloured up with shame;
It made him wince to own a Prince
Of very famous fame.

'He looked for one with speed and strength
And youth, and picked on me at length
And ordered me to stand
Prepared to leave at break of day,
With letters naught must long delay,
For certain cities far away
Across this lonely land.

'He told me all the roads to take
And cautioned me to go
With ears and eyes and wits awake,
Alert from top to toe,
For spies and thieves wore out most shoes
Upon the roads that I must use,
As he had cause to know.

'I took my cloak as morning broke
And started down the hill,
With Castle-bells and Fare-ye-wells
And bugles sweet and shrill —
Sir Woodman, though it's months ago,
I hear that music still.

'What matters now or ever how
I made the journey here!
I fed on berries from the bough,
Abundant everywhere,
Or if it failed, that luscious meat,
I dug up roots that wild hogs eat
And flourished on the fare;
At night I made a grassy bed
And went to sleep without a dread
And woke without a care —

'No matter how I managed now,
It all went well enough,
Until I saw this spot, I vow,
No man was better off.

'Last night as I came down this vale
In wind and rain full blast,
I turned about to hear a shout,
"Ho, master, whither so fast!"

'A minute more and half a score
Of men were at my side,
Plain merchants all, they said they were,
And camping in a thicket near,
"Remain with us!" they cried.

' "Remain with us, our board is spread
With cheer the best, Ah, stay," they said,
"Why go so proudly by!"
And there and then my legs were lead,
A weary man was I!

'They stared with wonder that I walked
These tangled hills and dales, and talked
Of better roads at hand,
Smooth roads without a hill to climb
A man could walk in half the time,
The finest in the land,
With more, — but most of it I lost
Or did not understand.

' "So, come," they cried, "our tents are tight,
Our fires are burning warm and bright!
How shall we let you go to-night
Without offending Heaven!
Come, leave you shall with morning light,
Strong with the strength of seven!"

'True men they seemed, for me I dreamed
No whit of their design,
Their mildness would have clapped a hood
On sharper eyes than mine;
Ay, me they pressed awhile to rest,
Persuaded me to be their guest,
And stole the letters from my breast
When I fell down with wine!

'It all came crowding on my mind
With morning when I woke to find
How blind and blind and utter blind
And blind again I'd been;
Both tents and men had vanished then,
Were nowhere to be seen.'

'Twas word for word a tale I'd heard
Not once or twice before,
Since first I made an axe ring out
Upon the timber hereabout,
But twenty times and more.

For many a year we've harboured here
A nest of thieves and worse,
Who watch for these young Castlemen
At night among the gorse,
It's hard to say if one in ten
Gets by with life and purse.

I wonder since 'twould serve the Prince
To square accounts with these, —
And many a score of footpads more
All like as pins or peas,
Who ply their trades in other glades
And plunder whom they please —
He does not rout the vermin out
And hang them to the trees.

But this poor lad — for me I knew
Scarce what to think or say,
I pitied him, I pitied, too,
Those cities far away.

I asked him would he stay and be
A woodman in these woods with me,
Perhaps he did not hear,
Perhaps the dove in song above
Beside its mistress dear
Was Castle-bells and Fare-ye-wells
And hornets in his ear;
An old gray man in all but years,
He pulled his cloak about his ears,
And went I know not where.

The Swallow

THE morning that my baby came
They found a baby swallow dead,
And saw a something, hard to name,
Flit moth-like over baby's bed.

My joy, my flower, my baby dear
Sleeps on my bosom well, but Oh!
If in the Autumn of the year
When swallows gather round and go ——

A Wood Song

Now one and all, you Roses,
  Wake up, you lie too long!
This very morning closes
  The Nightingale his song;

Each from its olive chamber
  His babies every one
This very morning clamber
  Into the shining sun.

You Slug-a-beds and Simples,
  Why will you so delay!
Dears, doff your olive wimples,
  And listen while you may.

Reason has Moons

REASON has moons, but moons not hers
  Lie mirror'd on her sea,
Confounding her astronomers,
  But, O! delighting me.

       *   *   *

BABYLON— where I go dreaming
When I weary of to-day,
Weary of a world grown gray.

       *   *   *

GOD loves an idle rainbow
No less than labouring seas.

The Bride

THE book was dull, its pictures
As leaden as its lore,
But one glad, happy picture
Made up for all and more;
'Twas that of you, sweet peasant,
Beside your grannie's door —
I never stopped so startled
Inside a book before.

Just so had I sat spell-bound,
Quite still with staring eyes,
If some great shiny hoopoe
Or moth of song-bird size
Had drifted to my window
And trailed its fineries —
Just so had I been startled,
Spelled with the same surprise.

It pictured you when springtime
In part had given place
But not surrendered wholly
To summer in your face;
When still your slender body
Was all a childish grace
Though woman's richest glories
Were building there apace.

'Twas blissful so to see you,
Yet not without a sigh
I dwelt upon the people
Who saw you not as I,
But in your living sweetness,
Beneath your native sky;
Ah, bliss to be the people
When you went tripping by!

I sat there, thinking, wondering,
About your life and home,
The happy days behind you,
The happy days to come,
Your grannie in her corner,
Upstairs the little room
Where you wake up each morning
To dream all day — of Whom?

That ring upon your finger,
Who gave you that to wear?
What blushing smith or farm-lad
Came stammering at your ear
A million-time-told story
No maid but burns to hear,
And went about his labours
Delighting in his dear!

I thought of you sweet lovers,
The things you say and do,
The pouts and tears and partings
And swearings to be true,
The kissings in the barley —
You brazens, both of you!
I nearly burst out crying
With thinking of you two.

It put me in a frenzy
Of pleasure nearly pain,
A host of blurry faces
'Gan shaping in my brain,
I shut my eyes to see them
Come forward clear and plain
I saw them come full flower,
And blur and fade again.

One moment so I saw them,
One sovereign moment so,
A host of girlish faces
All happy and aglow
With Life and Love it dealt them
Before it laid them low,
A hundred years, a thousand,
Ten thousand years ago.

One moment so I saw them
Come back with time full tide,
The host of girls, your grannies,
Who lived and loved and died
To give your mouth its beauty,
Your soul its gentle pride,
Who wrestled with the ages
To give the world a bride.

After

'How fared you when you mortal were?
  What did you see on my peopled star?'
'Oh well enough,' I answered her,
  'It went for me where mortals are!

'I saw blue flowers and the merlin's flight
  And the rime on the wintry tree,
Blue doves I saw and summer light
  On the wings of the cinnamon bee.'

The Skylark

THE world of old that stopped and stared,
With simple wits revolving
The singer and the song, declared
The riddle past resolving.

A later skylark takes the sky,
A wiser world lies under;
And still we put our wisdom by
And give the bird our wonder.

But, ah! within our inmost ear
Some pit of sense is ringing
With new surmise that more we hear
Than mortal skylark singing, —

That muffled in his shrill amours
Another voice is speaking,
That access there is surely ours,
Ours surely for the seeking.

Our dusts are one; we dare to think
Us destined to one glory;
For more: by faith alone we link
Two chapters of one story.

His but to be and sing and soar —
So but the skies invite him —
As he all day and evermore
Would in his lung delight him;

To own before his sovran sun
No lowly tie or tether
Beyond the fair that dotes upon
His crest of pointed feather;

To leap anew and lost within
The beams and blue abysses
Enchant her with redoubled din
Of benisons and blisses,

And flutter fainting from the sky —
His frenzy past and over —
Into her poppied bowery
Or shock of ruddy clover,

And make her bridal bed between
The boles of pipy grasses
Or in a maze of scented green
And secret ports and passes;

To pay the world nor tax nor toll
Save with his melic labours,
To claim in turn nor due nor dole
Save peace and gentle neighbours;

To hoard no boon beyond his wing,
No bauble but his beauty,
His but to be and soar and sing
And wave his dear his duty,

And shout him blest and over-blest
Until the skies reject him,
And hear the while within his breast
No privy woe correct him;

To ken no thorn offending there,
No new, no ancient fester
With stubborn smart his years despair
To soften or sequester,

No burnings for a bygone day,
No bodings of hereafter,
No wounds like them we hide away
Beneath our smiles and laughter.

Sun-climber he, his ladders run
Through spaces ever sparkling!
We make no song and climb no sun
But ways within us darkling;

How dark we know, how utter dark,
When blundering heels beside us
Crush out some timely watchet spark
Of glow-worm dropt to guide us;

Or when some fenny match ablaze
One sudden moment sighted
As sudden leaves our dazzled gaze
And us the worse benighted.

Yet are we blest: we know we climb
From darker ways behind us,
That suns will break for us in time
Too early broke would blind us,

And lit within we'll stand among
The corn at last receiving
The secret of our skylark's song,
And more we go believing.

The Weaving of the Wing

HER seas and mountains made,
Her skiey labours done,
A new design was hers.
She called a sprite and said
'Go up into the sun
And draw me gossamers.'
He brought a hundred strands,
Sun-yellow, to her hands.

She called her weavers up.
A wild burst into bloom;
Above a flaming whin
She hung a shallow cup,
Her weavers, silk and loom
And law she laid therein,
And turned and kept her way
An aeon and a day.

As down the wild I came,
This day, the crown of Spring,
I tapped a knotted spray
Above a whin aflame,
And saw a ribboned wing,
Sun-yellow, slip away
And hand and eye confessed
A young-forsaken nest.

I let my lips rejoice
I cried 'The work is done',
And praised the weavers' skill.
Thereat I heard a voice:
'The work is but begun,
My weavers labour still,
Not yet the warp and woof
They render question-proof.

Look in the nest again.'
I deeper looked therein,
I saw her silk of sun,
Her loom and weavers plain,
And heard a muffled din
And knew a web begun —
The warp and woof whereof
At last she will approve.

Ay, this I surely know:
An aeon and a day
From this, the crown of Spring,
As down the wild I go
I'll tap that knotted spray
And start a yellow wing!

'The work is done' I'll hear
And let my lips rejoice,
'Is done' I'll echo there
The Universal Voice.

I Love a Hill

TO JAMES STEPHENS

I LOVE a hill for in its hands —
If it's a friendly hill —
I can get back to magic lands
Of boyhood when I will.

And I can ramble ages vast
Before me and behind :
Reach sounding cities of the past,
Now dust upon the wind,

Then turn my back on ages old
And watch the forest creep
On London Town, the wild lay hold
On Paul's, a toppled heap.

And I can stay at home and find
The hill itself content my mind,
And sup on wonders still . . .
I love a hill for twenty things,
I always take a road that brings
Me halt upon a hill.

To a Linnet

NAY, preen again thy painted breast
And preen thy wing,
No menace to thy folded nest

Or thee I bring,
I come upon thy whin and weed
To hear thee sing.

Because a near and heavy need
To sing is mine,
I bring an immelodious reed

To school at thine.
A lucky hour finds Fate at fault,
Fate most malign,

Its end must fall with dread assault,
Shift how I will.
Sweet master, teach me to exalt

My coming ill,
Teach thou my pipe while learn it may
Some little skill,

For I that fear and cannot stay
The poisoned whip,
Would know with song to put away
A craven lip.

To Deck a Woman

(HAROLD HODGE REMEMBERED)

1

I KNOW a place of summer doves,
Rapt lizards in its alleys lie,
And mostly there a linnet loves
To mend a wanting melody.

No men talk there; no pit or gin
Trips Beauty on that sunny hill;
Its voice is ever gracious din
Of bee and song-bird never still,

And anthem yet from other quires :
The muffled diapason gushed
From lips occult and privy lyres
And pipes of Eden never hushed —

The pipes and lyres and lips that are
In sods and bubbles, stones and trees
And flying seeds from woodlands far
And wandering airs and essences.

Within, about, above, below,
Sprites elemental, Night and Day,
And winds and thunders, frost and snow
And wild things only, know their way.

2

And there I seek like any bee,
When skies are kind or do no wrong,
Such sweets as I may gather me,
Soothe charities of hue and song.

There, late, a linnet dipped; I saw
Him smooth his rimpled smock and then
The pathos of his eager straw
Got me the words I give my pen:

One melody, one lustre lost,
One loveliness of Earth at end —
Not Heaven deflowered of all its host
Were deeper wound or worse to mend.

And there mine edge of sense fell blunt,
Such poppy in the sun it found;
Of Beauty winging as she wont
I saw no more, nor heard a sound.

3

Among the briars newly blown
I saw two women fair to see,
No more than girls to women grown,
Of grace beyond hyperbole.

I might have looked on sisters here,
So close their comely charms agreed,
But plainly these no sisters were,
Nor cousin kith nor aught a breed.

A lovely Earthling all confused,
All wills and woulds and wits awry,
Surprised and spelled by one, I mused,
She feared alike to face or fly;

By one whose barbèd glances stole
Into the very veins of her,
Beneath the shutters of her soul
And through its shrouded theatre.

'Well met', quod I, for soon enough
I saw what matter filled her mind
Who, shammed an hour in mortal stuff,
Was come to chop with mortal kind.

She told a plain adventure plain —
Dissembled nothing, nothing dyed,
Indulged no idle antic vein —
And nothing told or touched beside.

4

'O stranger, know . . .
Earth's loveliness is shrunken low,
Its cry am I . . .

When I at first made Morning fall
On this my world of fell and flood
And saw its face how fair, withal
How short of fair the solitude,

I bade the rainbow clasp the sod,
The hills and dells put forth their green,
The wort and willow break the clod,
The daisy and the palm be seen;

And cried into the sinks and seas
On flocks unfashioned, droves in dream,
And led them to the dews and trees
And evening star and morning beam;

And made them fair with fleece and mane —
As well the meek and slow for mark
As them of fiercer, prouder strain,
The masterbreeds that left the dark —

And fair with lustrous quill and song —
The lowliest and least to rise
No less than them the first among
The hosts ambitious for the skies.

5

O happy lawns of Eden Star
When all a rainbow-haunted day
The treetop quires made melic war
With master-lay on master-lay,

And shrill hosannas of the lark
Flowed down unceasing from the sky
Till night came over gilt and dark
And hushed the lists of melody;

When ghost owls in the branches flew
As silent as the moony air,
And foxes ran among the dew
And forest eyes shone everywhere;

And sadding-sweet of nightingales
And catches of the babble-wren
Came from the woods and willow vales,
O happy lawns of Eden then!

6

Ay, fox and dove I made them fair;
Unseen, unseeing, senseless, null —
I made them of my world aware
And taught them to be beautiful.

Albeit then I turned mine eyes
To glooms and fires and spaces far
In gassy plight, and shining skies
Unkenned upon my peopled star,

114

Mine ear I turned not whole away —
What rat among the rushes stirred
Or fox forefled the break of day
Or blue dove sang, but him I heard!

The eagle winnowing the height
Pennipotent; the brindled moth
Or moon he fanned or phosphor light
Of julus curved, I heard them both.

Loud thrush or ever tree was green,
Lone robin when the tree was bare,
The sough and hum and song between,
The wing and wild pipe everywhere,

The mocks and laughs and strepent cries
And challenges and voices small,
Shy dove-notes and dulciloquies
And mutterings immusical,

I heard them each and every one;
No linnet red to breathe a note
But with red linnet blithe upon
The yellow whins of worlds remote,

Sang morning joy and evening cheer
And delectation else among
The central woodlands of mine ear —
The Bourne of universal song.

7

And well and sweet my linnets sang,
But morning broke in Eden sky
When lay and lovesong fainter rang
Down dwindled quires of melody;

When step and start among the trees
And voices new and strange to hear,
Fell sounds and foreign silences,
Affronted and perplexed mine ear;

When low to loud the clamour rolled
And low to loud past clue and key,
Anon, anon like naught of old,
Anon, anon to riddle me.

8

I pondered Eden — In the height
And in the deep no fairer star.
The honey did like aloe bite,
The grape was crab with vinegar.

I saw me by some destin dark
Defeated of mine honest flower,
My garden sunk in stupor stark,
An upas bough in Eden bower,

In Eden fen a lidless eye
Of basilisk on Beauty thrown —
And fable-stuff and fantasie
The like and turned to clay mine own —

Some monstrous fry of mortal seed
Than aught in story lewder far,
Some tall ambitious masterbreed
Supplanted me on Eden Star;

Some prospered vein, I mused, of bloods
Myself misgrafted in the sloughs,
Long ere I led the multitudes
To Eden's painted sods and boughs;

Or folly of my prentice hand
Among the streams, or ever sea
Or sod I made or Eden planned,
Returned with fatal fruit on me.

9

So I came out; disputing still,
Bemused, all minds at large between
Obscure and apprehended ill,
I lighted on my plot terrene.

I met no happy flocks among
The fastnesses of snow or sea,
Bad quiet in the boughs of song
And sunny places waited me.

10

I came with dawn a viewless shade
And waited in the April wood,
When every bough and every blade
And all the world on tip-toe stood;

When Winter fled a waxing sun —
His airy hosts and arms surpassed,
His rimy toparchs every one
For all their mettle cowed at last.

No gray thrush sang that skiey rout,
His branch was dumb, without a cry;
The wood and all the world about
Went silent in that victory.

11

And every sky was blue and rain
And sudden rainbows in between,
And every bough in leaf again
And all the world was gilt and green;

And all the world was bells and may
And sugared airs and leaping grass;
And every bough was flashed and gay
And all a dewy riot was;

And milks and wines ran fast and free,
And every cup was open wide
To every swarth or saffron bee
And every pictured wing beside;

And morning was a flaming brand
And eve a poppy late and long,
And lovetime was upon the land
And all the wood was sick for song.

12

I wandered aimless in the leaves,
All bracken birds and ribboned wings
And babble-dawns and lyric-eves
And reveries of perished things.

I saw the wood all trailing bowers
And boundless summer green above —
Ah, swathen all in summer flowers
Still waiting for their summer dove!

The bees and glassy things of air
And shardy flies and moths and shells
With horns and muffled musics there
Abounded as the honey bells.

For me their endless sough and hum
Was anthem vain, I got no sound.
For me the wood was stricken dumb,
The wood and all the world around.

I saw the wood in sweet and stale,
The shock and show and heavy crown,
The milks and wines come full and fail,
The glory dashed and all hung down,

The havoc winds, the clash and fall,
The shadow of the winter cloud;
I saw the wood — I saw it all,
The revelation and the shroud.

13

I found the pool broke up for Spring,
A wrinkled mock of flying sky,
Its wickered spume still glittering
With Winter's hoary charactry.

I watched and saw the first green spear
To leave its bed and breathe and be,
Grow fathom tall, and watched a year
Without a quill to gladden me.

When gray gnats came, and people kin
With minim shalms from cleft and clay,
To pasture once and whirl and spin
And perish with their natal ray —

When suns burned whole in pool and sky
Or bleeding lay; when every breath
To shake a reed and wander by
Confused a heaven of stars beneath —

When moths flew there and dragonflies,
Gold, blue, and green like scorchèd brass,
With tigered loins and opal eyes
Pursued their shades across its glass —

When pool and sky no longer paired,
When mist and thunder rolled between,
And tempest rocked and lightning bared
A pool of foam and crying green —

When dragonflies no longer flew
And reed and sedge hung down their ranks,
And chilly winds inconstant blew
The horns of Winter round its banks —

When frigid airs and bodies hoar
Laid hold upon its surges dark,
And blank it lay, the blaze of yore,
A glistering void without a mark —

And when the sedge stole back and through
Its beaded waters rainbow-shot,
And suns burned whole and bled anew,
I sought my birds and found them not.

14

I watched by night and listened still
With morning wetfoot in the grass
Of many a green sun-fondled hill,
And there that wounding silence was.

And high and low, and far and near,
Betimes with light, with shadow late,
Oft, oft and oft and everywhere
I met that hush importunate.

I turned away from carven trees
And scented shocks at thy own door,
From lichened eaves and lattices,
And saw the English isle no more.

I ranged my Star, the piny slants
And tilted earths and granites tall,
Green hills and sulph'rous adamants,
Dead pyres and pumice ashes all;

The snows and frozen sods and sands
Of dearth eternal; ever spare
And fitful green and milky lands
Of green abundance never bare.

I found the world forelet, forlorn:
The mountain woods and ledges forced,
The raven from the valley torn,
The eagle from the sun divorced.

I saw how drooped and dull and few
The wings upon the salted floods,
How fugitive and silent flew
The winglets in the honey woods;

How shrunk and flat the populace
That sparkled once upon the fen,
How oft assembled in the place
Of wings ten thousand less than ten.

15

I turned from Beauty's wounds to know
His look and air whose work they were,
What like the hand that brought her low,
The arm that surely strangled her;

What paramount of brute and bird —
The taloned dove within the tree,
The monstrous horn among the herd —
Disputed for my world with me.

121

A widowed fox with smothered bark
Foretold his foot, and hid in fear,
A bird uneasy in the dark
Declared him come or crouching near.

I saw him bowed beneath a load
Of carrion heads and eyes and wings,
And down his breast and shoulders flowed
The blood of doves and dying things.

16

I saw him oft, on every side
And everywhere and face to face —
It was upon a lotus tide
Or in some cassiad Asian place,

Or on the Lappish snow we crost
To meet anew by Niger flood,
Or on some ledge Andean lost
In cloud and snowy solitude,

Or in some ample, attar'd isle
Green even to the drowsy foam —
I met him with his burthen vile
Wherever Beauty made her home.

17

I saw him oft and saw him whole :
His ready eye and outward air,
The charnel place that was his soul,
His stupor in the twilight there;

His endless craft and patience in
A hundred trials of the chase;
His tireless foot so sure to win
The longest and the sternest race;

His learned use of hook and spike,
Of shaft and bolt and this and that
And every loath'd invention like,
And noisomeness I know not what.

18

I saw him whole and all he did
Of shame upon my hapless Star;
But neither from my sight was hid
His consort and familiar,

Who, lapped in lewdness viler made
By plenteous grace of lip and limb,
Crept sanctuaried in his shade
And ever close attended him;

Whose avid "More!" and "More! yet More!"
Urged every bout of shame and blood,
Or lovesick hern he ravaged for
The tassels of its lustihood,

Or finch or lark with lyric lung
He broke upon a scented hill,
Or crying seal he flayed and flung
To crimson waters crying still,

Or erne he humbled in the height,
Or fox beneath a pine trapanned,
Or raced and tripped some foot in flight
Across the snow or desert sand,

Or in the jungle found a prize,
Some shadow sleek of tawny hue,
Some forest thing with frightened eyes
Across the pool at night he slew.

123

19

A thousand irised winglets mine,
A thousand forest joys and fays,
Blusht arcs and fans shot berylline
And pied and purple, held his gaze;

He gathered sweets to load her lap
Whose faithful tireless hind he was,
And turned to watch new boughs and trap
In uninvaded areas.

A thousand homes of seal and stoat,
Of mew and tern rejoiced his reins —
A thousand sweets to glut the throat
Of Bloodwant shrill for Beauty's veins.

In her dread name he limed the bough,
In her dread name — Ah! serving thee
He broke the song in blood, for thou
And thou alone art surely she!

For thee he dragged his shambles through
The forests of my burning land,
In my insulted snows I knew
A labour of thy privy hand.

I knew thee in the sweet he laid
Beneath the western greenwood tree,
And in the hookèd spit he made
To redden in the winter sea.

With thine own fingers white and fair
He daubed the tangles of the south,
And blandished Beauty to the snare
With love-calls made by thy red mouth.

The airs and winds all tongues and ears
From wood and snow and desert shame,
And gusts and quaking atmospheres
Of foul'd savannas, say thy name.

Ten thousand voices name thee vile,
Earth's miscellany of tongues complete —
Her buds and herbs and cups that smile
In gold profusion round thy feet,

Her jungle deeps and mountain pines
And pastures and green places all,
Becks, pools and streams and billow-brines
And mists that on their faces fall,

Her flying clouds and skies above,
Her granite thews and undercrusts —
Her myriad pulses weary of
The lewd delights and carrion lusts.

22

Armipotent thou art and wise
And strong of seed; for me, I bring
No threat or thought of just reprise
To curb thy much ambitioning.

I have no sleight to match with thine,
No arms to give thee open war;
I mean no panic anodyne,
No ease for my distempered Star.

Its season-blind unshifting Law,
The same my being joined on me,
What hour I mused and willed and saw
The starry birth, will shelter thee.

Then bring thou yet more learned guile
To sweeter poison surer still,
A swifter bolt to engine vile,
And work on Eden World thy will.

Put forth and deeper soil thou me;
Despised by thy own native grace,
By all things wild and fair and free
Abhorr'd and shunn'd, pursue the chase.

Lead Echo on from cry to cry
Of creature snared or hunted down,
Until the stammering hills reply
In concert last to Beauty thrown,

And paramount indeed thou stand,
The circle of thy shame complete;
The last red labour of thy hand
In bloody welter at thy feet.

23

Then shall the sod where Beauty fell
Send up her wraith in murrain guised
And in its clasp thy breed unhell
My paradise unparadised.'

Silver Wedding

In the middle of the night
He started up
At a cry from his sleeping Bride —
A bat from some ruin
In a heart he'd never searched,
Nay, hardly seen inside:

'Want me and take me
For the woman that I am
And not for her that died,
The lovely chit nineteen
I one time was,
And am no more' — she cried.

Old Words

—Say that over!
'The loved one and the lover.'
— Words now one never hears;
Once more over —
'The loved one and the lover.'
—Strange they sound to modern ears!

Shepherd's Warning

(25 January 1794)

QUEER weather, thought the twite:
Sharp weather, feared the twite:
Foul weather, warned the twite
And fled the hills so bare of thorn —

Made off while it was light,
Before he lost the light,
While the sheepbells tinkled lightly
On the hills where he was born.

The shepherds took the warning
And made all haste to go
But gave it up for snow,
Lay down at last in snow and slept
Among the sheep till morning —

No sheep out that night
Or sheepdog out that night
Or shepherd out that night but slept
And overslept next morning.

The Pansy

I've looked as far as I can see —
Though that's not far — down into me;
If you have seen as much of you
And tell me it's a pretty sight,
Look again, and take a light.

On second thoughts don't trouble to,
You may be right —
And where's my introspection now?
I missed that pansy in the slough.

To Hang a Man

To hang a man:
To fit the cap,
And fix the rope,
And slide the bar,
And let him drop.
I know, I know:
What can you do!
You have no choice,
You're driven to;
You can't be soft —
A man like that;
But Oh it seems —
I don't know what —
To hang a man!

Hymn to Moloch

O THOU who didst furnish
The fowls of the air
With loverly feathers
For leydies to wear,
Receive this Petition
For blessin an aid,
From the principal Ouses
Engaged in the Trade.

The trouble's as follows:
A white-livered Scum,
What if they was choked
'Twould be better for some,
S'been pokin about an
Creatin a fuss
An talkin too loud to be
Ealthy for us.

Thou'lt ardly believe
Ow damn friendly they are,
They say there's a time
In the future not far
When birds worth good money'll
Waste by the ton
An the Trade can look
Perishin pleased to look on,

With best lines in Paradies
Equal to what
Is fetchin a pony
A time in the at,
An ospreys an ummins
An other choice goods
Wastefully oppin
About in the woods.

They're kiddin the papers,
An callin us names,
Not Yorkshire ones neither,
That's one of their games,
They've others as pleasin
An soakin with spite,
An it dont make us appy,
Ow can it do, quite!

We thank thee most earty
For mercies to date,
The Olesales is pickin
Nice profits per crate,
Reports from the Retails
Is pleasin to read;
We certainly thank thee
Most earty indeed.

Vouchsafe, then, to muzzle
These meddlesome swine,
An learn em to andle goods
More in their line,
Be faithful, be foxy
Till peril is past,
An plant thy strong sword
In their livers at last.

Time

Spiralwise it spins
And twirls about the Sun,
Both with and withershins
At once, a dual run
Anomalously one;
Its speed is such it gains
Upon itself: outsped,
Outdistanced, it remains
At every point ahead,
No less at all points led,
At none with either strains
Or lapses in the rush
Of its almighty vanes
To mar the poise or hush;
Comparing it for speed:
Lightning is a snail
That pauses on its trail
From bank to underbrush,
Mindful of its need,
With dawn astir, to feed
Before the morning thrush;
Comparing it for poise:
The tops we spun to sleep,
Seemingly so deep
Stockstill, when we were boys,
No more than stumbled round,
Boxwoods though they were,
The best we ever wound
Or whipped of all such toys;
Comparing it for sound:
The wisp of gossamer
Caught in a squirrel's fur,
Groans like a ship aground;
Shadow makes more noise.

'There is a Lady' —

On the threatened return
Of a bodily ill,
Long absent enough
To quiet concern,
But mischievous still
I now was to learn,
The strangest thing happened —
I caught myself singing!
— Me, in the mopes
With a decade of hopes
To forget — never less
In the mood: but the song,
'There is a Lady',
Changed that before long;
I don't say it rid me
Of cause for distress:
I do that it doctored me
Up into shape
To stand an assault
I was not to escape:
That good it did me:
I couldn't say how,
But it did — by some virtue
Or charm in its air —
In its portrait, so taking —
Its passion, full flare
At first sight — in its vow
Of such singular beauty —
That ditty divine
Which an olden-days Lover
Sang to his Lady;
— Did, and does now
As I sing it to mine
Over and over.

The Hever Picnic

SHOCK howled: the merry buzz stopped dead:
All but Anne went terrified,
As round the bush at a tall man's stride
        Came Luckie Lee,
            Queen of the Egyptians.

Anne, cutting her a slice of pound-cake, said:
'Why d'you stare so — what d'you see!
'Staring like a hawk at me,
'Good woman?'
            'H'm', their guest replied,
'Weddings . . . beddings . . . and . . .'
               'And what?'
The lovely Bullen begged.
              'And that

'Is all, as far as I can see',
And — muttering to herself aside:
'Not for both her silver bracelets' —
Round the bush at twice the stride
        Went Luckie Lee,
            Queen of the Egyptians.

Tobit

THE book says: 'So they went forth both,
  'And the young man's dog went with them.' —
                              Name
Not told us —
                    'So they went their way
'And the dog went after them.'
                              That's all;
Not a word of breed or build,
Coat, colour, age, sex — anything!
                    Had I but lived in Nineveh
And met them on the road!
                              Some night,
Unless my dreams give out. . . .
                              'Oh, Sirs,
  'Pray pardon me' —

Of Nature, write —

BULL to the cow,
Boar to the sow,
Cock to the hen
On the blossoming bough:
There's nothing in Her world
To foul the fair pen
Of an innocent Muse:
She keeps no stews;
So write of Her; tell
That all's Eden and well:
No sniggers or smirks
At sight, sound or smell
Affront Her chaste Works;
She never fell.

To-day

I HEAR the saddest sounds to-day,
I cannot turn my ears away;
The world's sick to death, they say . . .

'Summer — Autumn — Winter — Spring!'
(It's the chaffinch cock in the lilac tree)
'Summer — Autumn — Winter — Spring!
'Hi! Where's that hen for me?'

I see the saddest sights to-day,
I cannot turn my eyes away;
The world's sick to death, they say . . .

'Summer — Autumn — Winter — Spring!'
(It's the chaffinch cock in the lilac tree)
'Summer — Autumn — Winter — Spring —
'And here's that hen for me!'

The Smile

PICTURE him sinner —
Picture him saint —
A man without honour —
A man without taint —
It is but a picture
It pleased you to paint —
He knows how false,
How far from the life,
As nobody else,
Not even his wife.
— Why must you smile?

The Foreman Said:

'WE'RE all in agreement, then; before
'We send this creature to his doom
'Or what the Court may have in store,
'Allow me to ask pardon from
'The wretch I, too, may yet become
'With bodily change, if nothing more,
'To exercise a jury room
'As briefly . . . Now we'll tap the door.'

To Vegetate—

        To vegetate
's to live at a terrific rate :
Pinks drudge like slaves : a lotus lives
A navvie's life : a hazel nut
's a power-house : a runner bean
A rope-walk; it's the grind to grow
As much as slaving in the heat
That throws a sunflower into sweat;
'Pity, but it has to go' —
Lilies do toil;
From a bed of phlox in blow,
Butterflies work as hard as bees.

'The Ousel Cock'—

I ASKED a cock blackbird,
'Why did you choose black?
'— In the ages of old
'When blackbirds were new
'And questions of hue
'Began to unfold —
'With the rainbow to choose from,
'Why did you pick black?'

'You mean', he replied,
'That a blackbird's no posy . . .
'But that point aside;
'This charge that we slighted
'The rainbow of old:
'Are you nearsighted?
— 'Black goes with gold
'In a manner that dizzies
'Our hens to behold
'In the Spring of the year;
'That's why we chose black
'In the ages far back,
'And how we got here,
'If you need to be told.'

The Muse and the Mastiff

'For what can ail the mastiff bitch?'

*

J., living in the country, some distance from London, owns a mastiff bitch puppy five or six months old: latterly she has become subject to violent dreams at night, in the stable yard.

J., a bit puzzled, sends his friend R., a poet living in an attic in Chelsea, a postcard describing these dreams: his wife, a wider reader than he, adds the inevitable postscript.

R. at once interprets the dream by the theory of inherited experience, and the appearance of the Muse is instantaneous. This is the outline of an introductory portion of the poem, here omitted. The poem is presented as being read by R. to J. on a visit to the country, six weeks later.

SOMETHING of him still comes out
Of his moorland fog — some hazy, dim,
Old family death's-head print of him
In her blood and bones — and into sight,
Hoisting itself across the wall
And shuffling a hairy foot about
The shrubbery and paths at night,
In her sleep: Here, Now: a call
Precisely such as once upon a time
When he was in his fleshly prime
And she in hers — as still she is —
He paid upon the moorland villages,
Himself, the lost Original,
In certain of his moods, not all.
Not, for example, as he came
With a backward Easter, sulky, sour,
But shy of parish note and fame
And homesick almost from the hour;
His purpose — quiet meals and cheap —
How ever frail and insecure
On soil so rich in cattle and sheep,
Sustained by second thoughts ten deep
At every step: the first rebuff,

Or disappointment, up and off —
On to the village rubbish heap;
Not the pad to stand on pride
And suffer for a clocking hen,
Or stumble into mastiff ken,
Company less, and less again
Likely to enter that full stride —
Least of all round village doors
So distant from his mountain den —
And come, unless he played a part
That cut the road off at the start,
Buffeting his way through time and tide
A thousand years to threaten yours,
And mystify the best of men
And rush the Muse — in all her glow
And innocence of Ah, how long ago!
— Winged on one imperishable line
Of *Christabel* post-haste to mine,
Not for him that glory, then.

Only in his looks the bear:
Casting about the parish skirts
With less to eat than his deserts
Behind him for the time of year,
Or more than he could make his own
Among so many with his tastes,
And seldom with his tastes alone
But with his talents and to spare,
Beforehand with him everywhere
Up and down his gloomy wastes:
Every sort and shape and size
Of plundering jowl and beak they bred —
In seasons of abundance there
Hardly more than smells and cries
And shadows passing while he fed,
He on his rounds, they on theirs,

Trueing up all unawares
And forwarding the lustihead:
Hurrying the blood round hardly red
Or red too raw or red too ripe
Or red too many of a type —
When prick a wolf a bluecap bled,
Missing from its trysting tree,
And missing from its marsh a snipe —
Its moor a bull — its glade a bee —
Beck a minnow — mountain top
And circles to the setting sun,
With next to nothing in its crop
And half the forest in its veins,
An eagle — spirted in the drains.

That, for the most part, later on,
Come change of weather from the South:
Sunny showers and buttoned trees,
Dothery-grass up and a breeze
With smells in tow to start his mouth
A-watering for the rubbing stones
And wallows — shun them as he might,
And haunt them as he must despite
The sternest precepts of a bear:
No gaming with the bulls and boars
Apart from rheumy outcast ones:
Breakage of the fens and moors —
When duly peopled for the year,
And something better on his bones
Than weasels' meat — what little of that
They left his mouth to water at,
Those lithe - er - those - - lithe - er - er - er -
How very odd!

Thus the Muse: her troubled tones
Lifted in the forest gloom

That hung three-quarters of the room,
Its briar-trellised wall-paper
And window-boxes : all at once
Evoking hiccups, yawns and groans
And lusty belches in response —
To make no mystery, from the bear,
None other than himself : his lair
The corner cupboard, blithe and gay
With rosy Minton till he woke,
Then a disembowelled oak,
Between the walnut chiffonier
And doorpost, also in decay,
Lichened ruins now, all three —
And in a husky whisper, low
But loud enough to bring her glow
Full flush and halt her by his tree,
The groan : Those hairy leeches, Lass!
. . . Those hairy leeches in the grass —
She thanked him — making signs to me
To turn the locked-up cupboard key
And save ourselves a shower of glass,
Not before high time — the bear
Tumbling out of his lichened lair
Just as I regained my chair,
Thinking to himself . . .

We know the risk
And take it — How too utterly grotesque,
We hear you say and answer : Quite!
— An arrow loosened at a mark
Almost wholly in the dark,
But bear in mind his appetite
For kitchen stuff : the trips he'd made
Below the moorlands : calls he'd paid
Upon the village plums at night —
Or failed to pay : at what expense

Of strain upon his every sense
Whilst waiting on the wind or moon
To point the moment opportune,
No matter here, as down he goes
Late of an autumn afternoon
By a path he only knows,
And in about one-twentieth
The time he took to take a breath
Drops into the lowland plain
And follows dusk up Lovers' Lane
Listening . . . . . .
. . . . . . Tiffs and troths alike
Have aided him, his work is done,
The fondest couple in the dike
And last to go, at length have gone:
Only apple cores remain:
Only the owls and bats are out:
So, quicker than a fly can wink
Or spinnymidge turn thrice about,
Just as quick as he can think,
Up he comes with every word
Giggled, sobbed or sighed he'd heard,
Into his lichened lair again,
The ragbags of his memory
All in order now: well, then —
Thinking to himself: Who could she be?
Not young Maudlin from the Farm?
The freckled goose-girl, Mog? Nor she:
Nor Grizel from the ferry? No,
Nor Jennis from the mill below —
Hanging on her laddie's arm
The type of village bloom and charm —
The miller's daughter, like them all,
Talked with a twang and has to go . . .
Sweet Jennis . . . who, then, after her,
Unless some Missy from the Hall?

Or guest they entertained from Town!
A minx who knew her weasels, though,
And something of himself besides,
Something of what his sufferings were
This dreariest of Eastertides —
Some young Somebody come down
From Somewhere or other —

                              Anyhow,
Tumbling out of doors to bow,
Piqued to take the measure of one
So clearly above the common run
Of callers — mainly twenty-legs,
Wood-lice, devil's coach-horses,
Spiders, twitchbells, hornets, clegs,
Ticks and such — nay, even of these
Few stirring yet.

                     All said and done
Precisely as foreseen : the Muse
Mindful of how he swung his rump
On daylight for some hollow stump
Among the hoary oaks and yews,
And such to be met with by the score,
Delighting but not surprising me
By picking out the very clump,
Pausing at the very tree
And practising her innocent ruse
Just as the light, all day but poor
At that began to fail, and he
To rouse himself from lethargy.
Little blood-sots, always dry,
Always drinking!
                    Weasels?
                          Ay,
Weasels — not so hard as stoats,

However, 'twas only fair to say,
Or fitches by some pints a day
Or martens by as much again
And room for more than liquor then —
And nothing stuck in martens' throats
He'd noticed : hours he spent at night
Watching martens line their coats :
Where they managed to put it all —
What passed through 'em and out of sight
Apart — such creatures, only small,
Nothing of 'em, just a nip
Anywhere from tip to tip,
Was something quite beyond him, quite;
The failings of the weasel race
Were many, some proverbial —
He paused and sniffed and made a face —
Throughout the woods : he instanced those
Of polecats, to a squeamish nose —
Here a second, worse grimace —
The last offence : do what he would
Bide a fitch he never could,
Of all that thirsty class of beast
Fitches he respected least,
Fitches turned his stomach! She,
Connecting a certain pungency
With her robustious vis-à-vis,
To chide his disingenuousness
And want of heart : But how unkind!
Was it their fault if they stank?
And promptly on his replying, Yes,
They only had themselves to thank —
And doubtless did — retorting, Well,
If she could trust her sense of smell,
Even bears gave odours off!
He in his turn also frank :
Houts, Lass, yes, but not so rank!

Extending to her nose one paw:
Racy, perhaps, but sweet enough
He trusted . . . ? Now this other . . . Faugh!
Devil a bit the least like that
He needn't say, no more need she,
Now, knowing what misled her nose;
Which with her apology —
Something forced, a little flat,
For still she thought his words unfair —
Brought the quarrel to a close,
The Muse next door to tears, the bear
Brooding on the bulk and weight
And blessings he had lost of late
To other creatures everywhere
Between him and his proper share.

She spoke first: again at ease
In spite of mishap at the start,
With various learned treatises,
Tracts and journals, off by heart
To sustain her in her part,
And contributions of her own
To thought as timely, not a few —
Thanks to the Age of Print — well known:
Portraitures of bats and owls,
Ousel cocks and farmyard fowls,
Bees, bulls, boars and dumbledors,
Grasshoppers and crickets, true
As Bewick cuts; her pity shown
For all such creatures wronged: the rights
Of field-mice to their building sites,
Foggage, and an ear or two
Of corn, affirmed: astute remarks
On fleas, high starry things on larks
And earthworms: selfless, pious acts
Of emmets, moles and wrens revealed —

The British fauna's spiritual affairs
Commemorated with delight
In book upon book, all crammed with facts
Which other workers in the field,
From prejudice, perhaps, or oversight,
Omitted when presenting theirs;
Recent enough, all: nothing said
Of much still running in her head
That we lost hold of long ago,
For want of print to make it fast
Against the steady undertow
Of Time throughout the sunken past,
But famous when Stonehenge was new
And all the talk: of wide renown
In blocks of years yet deeper down,
Ever since — we pause at When,
But dig them up a bone or two
And leave the date to learned men —
Ever since the first young lad
Of proper parts we ever had
Listened to a lark and heard
Something other than the bird
And sat down dizzy . . .

                       She spoke first,
A little pensive at the worst:
She hoped he had a better word
For hedgehogs? He was far away.
Badgers? Not a syllable.
She trusted he had a word to say
For beavers? Still he seemed distrait.
Hedgehogs — badgers — beavers — well,
Otters? Otters broke the spell:
He had a compliment to pay
To otters — this he promptly paid:
Otters were a beast apart,
Unique for qualities of heart:

Otters, to her immeasurable delight,
Left him tails and sometimes more,
Depending upon the haste he made
To join them as they drew ashore —
Inestimably precious aid
Otters rendered in his plight;
Shyly she touched on cats, and true,
His compliments to cats were few,
To cats in kit, or kittled, none:
As few to foxes: he was hoarse
A-rowing them and wolves all night —

Wolves!
Of course, wolves: wolves, of course,
That clique: by comparison
Weasels were his bosom friends,
Skimping their little carcases
To spare him comforts — stoats the same,
Amity their only aim,
Struggling with their lusts to please
And fill him out with odds and ends,
Martens similarly employed,
Coddling him till dainties cloyed —
Fitches making what amends
They could by fasting till he'd fed —
Cats and foxes dropping dead
In sympathy — and then he'd said
Nowt . . .

So that was where he'd been?
Partly: always in the scene,
Wolves — though not the only thing —
Yowlying and yowlying,
Solo, trio, half a score
It might be, or as many more,

In winter all the louping pack
Up and down behind his back;
Rolling wolves took half his time
Once they scattered: danger lay
In picking on a wolf too soon,
Then he found a tree a boon:
A mercy that they could not climb . . .
Or fly . . . he broke into a sweat
At this thought . . . he was pleased to say
He had not idled in his day —
That very morning he had met
A couple from the carrs . . . but, there!
He had worse ills than wolves to bear . . .
His look was in the void again.

This last she thought a slap at birds:
He had not said a thing to show
His attitude to birds. Nor men,
Either, I added, not two words,
Yet he and they had been at odds
From very early periods;
I thought of marks he left below
In the heyday of his race —
She of Yarrell on the Crow:
The Carrion Crow, or Corbie, ate
Practically anything it could get:
A handsome bird, its character,
Everywhere accounted base,
Indeed had long been known to her . . .
A difficult problem was the age
We found him in . . . *The magpie, chough,*
Rook, raven, jay and jackdaw were,
As the illustrious Yarrell, pertinently enough,
Points out, all crows . . . Upon what page
Of Turner, Church or Collingwood —
Within what frame of time — we stood . . .

And well that writer's pen describes
The Buzzard, Kite and kindred tribes,
Their plumage, habits, tastes in food . . .
Was he early? Was he late?
Saxon, Roman or B.C.?
. . . . . . *Quite impossible to overrate*
His chapters on the Owl, a bird
To which she sometimes had referred
Somewhat, she feared, inaccurately . . .
Portentous one fact seemed to be:
Why no mention of a mate?
No hint of an associate
Or rival? Was he quite alone,
Of all his race the only one
Extant? If so, it fixed his date —
Norman times: the last bear fell,
If we could trust our reference,
While Rufus was upon the throne;
(I nudged her dimpled elbow:) *Well?*
(She heard me out) *A pair of wings*
Put him at a disadvantage: hence
His rancour, worst in backward Springs;
(She said, half glancing round to add
That Yarrell threw a blaze of light
On British birds, and she was glad
To profit by his sound good sense,
Deep study and experience:
Grateful, too, for Knapp and White
And others) . . . Did we dare assume
That threatened by approaching doom
He pierced the veil with second sight?
Some beasts appeared to have the power,
Why not he at such an hour?
— And if it went beyond his nose
Or half so far, indeed, why, then,
That explained his fling at men!

(She swung about without her crows)
Skipping over one report
That daubed the mild Confessor's court,
For want of detail — not of fact,
Another in the reign of John
I could not lay my hands upon
But somewhere among the litter stacked
About the shelves, and certain reigns
So far as I knew free from stains,
I spoke of blood-sick Marybone:
The Hockley pit: the Bankside hells:
Of Blackface and old Sackerson,
Scabby Hunks and others there,
Week in, week out, year after year
Unhutched amid the yawps and yells
And titters of the ghoulery —
To sweat the brows of God in Heaven,
And start a bead on London's even,
Smelling sin one day in seven —
And waited, trembling: as did she,
Scarlet to her scalp for me
And my repellent species: hers,
By adoption, not by blood
She meant it to be clearly understood,
Almost bursting into tears
With anger —

Croak . . . croak . . croak . . croak . . .
A homing carrion crow: the bird
Was opportune, it brought him to
And back to speech: For vice, Miss, yon!
He shot an arm out as he spoke,
(Not that the wrathful Muse withdrew
A blush, nor I a single word) —
But anything with feathers on,
Bar snipes and peewits and a few

That did on hayseed . . .

                              Birds of prey
Had been upon his mind all day:
Incredible amounts they ate;
That ring would make good its threat!
— Death bloodiest, and better dead
Than one more week of this, he said,
Talking to himself: she turned away
In colour: I, less delicate,
Looked wondering on — what passion stretched
His chaps to such a grin — what hate —
What frothing fury! (By his mouth
A bear, I gathered, past his youth)
Then fear — nay, horror now — he fetched
Such groans — again, what lusts! I watched
A trickle at his under lip
Repeatedly run dry and drip
And dry for good and all . . .

                              To go
At the bidding of a crow —
And leave his forests to a pack
Of eagles buzzards owls and pies
All for half a foot of snow!
His legs would give — the Beadle Bear
Would meet him on the moorland track
And retch, or pass him with a stare —
His mother's bony boggart rise
A-creaking from the shades below,
And urge him scourge him march him back
All gooseyflesh. No. Tell them, No.

Shyly the Muse looked up . . . To these —
Mainly bred at home, he said,
In inaccessible rocks and trees,
And plentiful enough to run him short,

Themselves alone, add winter flights,
Still in strength between the seas;
Regulars with forest rights
As good as his one half the year,
They boasted, deaf to his retort,
A mob of egg-bound fly-by-nights —
Scorn he flung at others there:
Strags and storm-blows still in port —
Salvage from the headland heights,
Whencesoever flown or blown,
Lost at sea and later found
By one another weather-bound
In billets at the wrong resort:
Beggary from roosts the round
Of gusty Europe, swept and thrown
Together on his patch of ground:
Howsoever diverse a throng
In point of feather, feature, frame,
Themselves, diverse again among
The native eagles buzzards crows
Owls hawks bitterns and gulls in those
And other respects, all one in aim —
All of a feather together the same
For anything he ever saw
Beyond the booty in the claw,
The plunder in the beak or bill,
Taken up and off at will
Almost from beneath his paw,
Stared he howsoever hard
At purple, tawny, blotched or barred
Or pepper-and-salt or piebald plume,
Or whatsoever spread of quill
Cuffed him blind for hours to come;
All of a hatch for thievish skill
And roomy crops in his regard
And purview — brooded out at home

In his next-door neighbour's nest
Or at the ends of Christendom,
Or under whatsoever breast —
All of an egg to his mind's eye
That judged by works not feathers best,
And lumped his neighbours with the rest
On evidence a full supply
Under almost any tree —
Ket and kin by any test,
Language one: whey-e-kee-wee,
Hek-hek, whoo-whoo or yelp or croak
Or scritch or whatsoever cry
Sounded from the first that woke
As darkness fell or daylight broke —
Starve him out, all, starve him out!
— From every quarter of the sky;
And would to the fates he too could fly
And fetch some bulging craws a clout!

Restitution from a crow
He had never had, nor from a raven
More than feathers back in kind:
Indeed, he failed to bring to mind
An instance of a jackdaw, even,
Letting more than feathers go
Or of a magpie's doing so;
In all, the crow tribes numbered seven:
It shocked him, the immense amount
Of sleep he lost on their account
Alone; of other birds of prey
Whose beaks were in his dish by day,
Up and down from every tree,
He said that devastation wrought
By species varied in degree,
Depending upon capacity
Of gullet — all with space to spare,

Always, driving him distraught.
— Spiders in like want and care,
Near enough if not four-square,
Solved his problem at the loom;
The little websters everywhere
Amazed him by the flies they caught;
The mystery was, where they managed to stow
Their plant and stock, so pinched for room
They seemed in contrast with a bear,
And how they made their jennies go;
'N the summer he gave much time and thought
To spiders, stopping for hours to stare :
Not only did it lighten gloom,
It worked him into such a glow
Of fancy as their prizes fought
Against the rigours of the snare,
Boding worse — all buzz and fume
Till quieted and trussed up taut,
That a body of eagles floundered there,
Knelling each its eyrie's doom;
In ecstasy his forearm brought
All but a mash of flies to naught.

                     .   .   .

Back again to the crow: for brains,
Ability to save its skin
Whatever straits it might be in,
And put on flesh at his expense —
Consistent all-round competence —
Commend him to the sinister bird
Whose tongue she had already heard
Some minutes back above that tree :
(Elsewhere, too, and long before,
Though after his time, paradoxically,
She could have told him, but forbore)
Considering them each and all in turn,
Though, none of them had much to learn

From him about its mother's trade
In those departments : classed as food,
Themselves, a source of livelihood,
A means of building up his flesh
And tallow, they were little aid :
Few he had ever tasted fresh :
Chicks and windfalls — seldom found,
The latter, he insisted, sound —
Aside, but few he'd ever seen
The breastbone of, for times he'd made
The effort in a misty glade
At dawn, or when they dropped to clean
And polish up their beaks and preen
Their feathers in the tricksy light
Of the gloaming, or at night,
And many, many as he'd laid
His paws on, even had between,
Blotted wholly out of sight
Of all and often as he'd been,
Convulsing the owls —
                              Beg pardon !
                                        Why,

He alluded to the owls : they went
Into fits of merriment
On these occasions.
                    Owls ! (Her cry
Was anger, all her soul ablaze,
But anguish too, and pity, blent
In one : without an easing sigh
Or tear she listened in a daze —
As, for seconds, so did I :)
Tomfoolery was not his bent,
(He was saying) Give him wit —
Talent — magpies jackdaws jays
Or crows, and he could cope or quit
And all good friends : od rabbit it,

He loved the vermin! But, (he said)
Save him from that dunderhead —
Born buffoon or crazy loon
At the mercy of the moon
And for its own sake better dead,
The scritching whowling whooting owl,
The dullest wits his forests bred,
Nature's rankest jobbernowl,
— He grinned: a bear must have his growl!

(The Muse was in a deathly swoon
Or next thing to it, near enough
To come to life with scorn, instead
Of sympathy and mild reproof.)
Owls of all birds, *owls* so free!
Such formal birds, such grave, aloof,
Unbending birds as *owls*! (To quote
Her own 'Tu-whoo, a merry note',
Was not my place) Fudge, fiddle-de-dee,
A roost of magpies! (Mine to bow
And write the dooming words: I wrote —
Cross, dejected: nothing now
Could save her from a clammy brow)
Emblems of rue and reverie
For eons! (Here she turned to me:)
At least I did not cock one ear
Then the other, then the pair
At every sound from miles around,
Distractingly as did the bear . . .
Sobriety itself so staid
As even fluffy owlets were!
Indeed, to watch a sitting hatch
And feather in their shroudy fir,
Unmoved as in the egg unlaid
By all the merry bustle and stir
The sparrows, spinks and buntings made

In earshot of its sombre shade
Had ever been a grief to her.
. . . .
So elderly at ten days old!
. . . . year
She took it to another tree,
As Winter, still in slattern snow,
Gathered up its skirts to go . . .
. . . An ivy-wrappered oak,
Ancient, gnarly, vast and squat . . .
Converted by some lightning stroke
Into a spacious owlet cot —
For anything that we could tell
Above us on that very spot,
In line direct with this old shell,
(Tapping his tree as she spoke)
Its acorn's acorn's acorn's butt,
And clouted from this selfsame cloak
(Twiddling an ivy spray)
Against the draughts of upper day
Here, too, was hatched a brood she watched
. . . .
With patience in her soul, and Knapp
On the Ivy in her lap . . .
. . . . . (sunshine) . . . .
Broke into the gloomiest wood
And put the brownest bush in green
A month before the hug of May
That spun the year in madcap mood
Dizzy to a pitch divine
And roses . . . But their ivy bower,
Under outside assault gave way,
Sagged so thin the sun broke in,
For its fruit, full flavour, out fullcrop
All up and down its sprawling spine
Had turned the autumn berries sour —

Remnants not yet in decline,
As, with rare prophetic power,
The misselthrush on the elmtree top
Had predicted from the hour
The Michaelmas buds burst into flower;
— Abundantly sufficient sign
That when the autumn fruits were spent,
Loads at Christmas for a hop
Along the hedgerows, juicy, fine
Full-bodied berries all — in Lent
A pittance for the miles he went,
No swallowing — then, that the family prop,
The February ivy berry,
Stanchion of his house and line
Of old, would be his strength and stay
And in beggarly March on March for aye.
So the misselthrush was at their bush
Beyond himself so blithe and gay,
Acting like a bird in wine,
Throwing tendrils out of twine,
Tugging and tearing spray from spray,
Fold from fold, till gaps between
Rendered void — practically destroyed
All that held the sun at bay,
And her owlets cowered from his brazen ray;
Sobersides and Woebetides,
Innocent of gall and spleen,
They looked, with little mouths drawn down
Into their chins, like cherubins
On monuments in marble brown
To persons of antique renown,
A mediaeval King or Queen
Or warrior: in such seemly art
She found their print and counterpart;
They came to feather in rainbow weather —
Benumbed by crises from the start

The merriment escaped them clean:
Never once the least response
To bless her eyes with had she seen:
For any feeblest faintest sound
Uncalled for by their humdrum round
Of duties, she had ever heard,
In the moon she might have been;
Twenty times her lashes drown'd . . .
Twenty times she dabbed them dry

. . . .

A-pitying bairns at that age bound
So fast to so severe a code
And wondering in sweet mercy, Why?
— She had not counted on the thought
That jerked her toes with its reply;
Yon selfsame body of laws had brought
Its charges up the owlet road
From Everlasting . . . Owlet Nought,
Hatch by hatch to that abode,
There to continue in the mode
Prescribed or perish . . . Brief, abrupt —
A lecture, and a lily lopped,
Breathing odours as it dropped!
— The mischief was she felt no shame:
If she had run a wayward course
Pious zeal for owlet weal
Had hushed misgivings at the source . . .
Looking back the ages through
At such variety of scene
On either side her path — how long!
— The circumstance was hardly new;
Listening to herself in song
From whatsoever source it drew —
Madonna or the Gipsy Queen
Or regions of the soul between,
Or whencesoever it had sprung

And swarmed the heartstrings to her tongue —
Not every note rang always true
To standards of the Golden Mean!
— Everlastingly so young,
Ten thousand years at Seventeen —
Longer, having all in view —
And always somewhat overstrung
In the Spring with everything
About her in a wild to-do,
A scatterbrain she *might* have been
But had she been a silly too,
Indulging like a mortal maid
In a maudlin escapade?
That a Muse could not excuse!
Answer was not long delayed:
All alive: a family of five,
They tumbled up and out that night,
In feather for a furlong flight,
Blithely, beautifully flown
Up and down the moonlit glade:
It all but broke her heart to own
How shadowy her grief had grown
In a twinkling, at the sight —

EPILOGUE

WELL we know that they made him pay
Then — or in his other shoes —
Dunned him till they got their dues,
Thus hastening his breed's decay
And fall into the winter sleep
That asks no tallow for winter keep:
Where only one mouth melts for prey
And clocks all stop or run to lose,

Never but a little while
Ticking to the tiny frets
Of Nature's last and smallest file:
But whether that night he stole away
Red with glory home again,
Leaving behind a load of debts
And bony dreams, or there and then
Paid his owings, who's to say?
Even your mastiff now forgets
Or only your mastiff knows to-day.

CORONATION DAY

10 December 1936

HE was a king and is:
Crown whom they must or may,
A crown is always his —
Of everlasting bay;
Here's a toast, then, up —
No malice in the cup —
Long live King Edward, he
Bloomed in rare majesty
On Coronation Day.

23 April 1937

★

PORTABLE WIRELESS

'MARRY? after listening to *that* — not I!'
That's the way our girls will talk
To-morrow on an evening walk
Comin' through the rye.

★

Listening in to Lud's time:
'*Flint prices rising. Unless the men on strike at Brandon
return to the mines within ten days, the owners . . .*'

★

. . . Don't forget
That the cowslip, rose and violet
Are Facts of Life, as well . . .

★

Outside,
Shameless Spring tells everything.

THE SNAIL

You never heard a snail in song?
Wait till the first thrush comes along.

★

'Skunks,' the squirrel said, 'are sent to try us.'

★

'Once you saw a blackbird
'With a halo round its head —
'You old liar!'
                        'It's what I said —
'At Pinner, in my twenties.'

★

The moth that loved a glow-worm woke up weeping,
To see the bony hag beside him sleeping.

★

Who shall paraphrase a tear!

★

THE CARDINAL

'It's beautiful to hear him —
But we girls - er - we - er - we -'
'You mean you'd rather wear him?'
'Ee-e-well-er-ee-hee-e-e.'

★

You can't rouge the spirit, Lady.

★

'Age, age,' groaned the hour-old midge,
'Can't do the twirls I did.'

★

The wink was not our best invention.

'You can't drive a bent nail home.'
— 'Twas Noah who first made that remark,
At the building of the Ark,
Waggling a bloody thumb,
And his delighted children's mirth
That gave the Comic Spirit birth.

*

. . . Innocent as my dog Patch,
        Barking at his echo . .

*

CHURCHILL

SOME back the Seer —
Others the Statesman —
Still others the Soldier —
To get the top honours
When no longer here,
And Time starts to cheer;
Rightly or wrongly
I'm backing the small boy
Of three score and ten,
Who put out his tongue
At the dread Mountain-den
In the days of the Fear;
— I fancy him strongly.

*

THE PEACE

AND now beware the tearful rogue
Who pities the tapeworm, not the dog.

*

When crises pall, humdrum is sensational.

EPIGRAM

How blessed is the little man
Who has a bigger brother,
Yet neither thinks himself a god
Nor deifies the other.

★

A sparrow in a snowstorm with a feather in his bill: that
is Faith.

★

Did you know, when you spurned Pity,
That Heaven was on its knees to you?
— That *HEAVEN* was on its knees to you —
That Heaven was on its KNEES to you —
That Heaven was on its knees to you,

Speck?

★

Oaths in anguish rank with prayers.

★

Some blamed the grate, some blamed the coal:
None blamed the choked-up flue:
And for want of a freshening draught of doubt
They let the Fire of Faith go out,
And the world stands shivering in its soul,
And they stand shivering too.

★

Love of God, the Madness,
In and out of season
Buttonholing everyone —
Love of God in reason:
Up to a point: upsetting none —
I have no turn for either
And side with neither:
By contrast, though, I do admire
The sanity of Blood and Fire.

★

171

Truth, it is feared, will yet prevail.
Facts are items: Truth's the sum:
There is no residuum.

*

Gently, Years, gently!

*

'False doctrine, and besides, it's new!'

*

'Old World, go when you wish,
'We Mod —'
          'So you were saying
'At Ur and Kish and Carchemish
'And Nineveh. I'm staying.'

*

If only Pilate could have kept his seat!

*

The Past comes back in the mouth with blood.

*

Forget the slush, but keep the snow
Of Christmasses of long ago.

*

Anniversary: Familiarity breeds content.

*

Dust thou Art, but dust carefully.

172

QUEER — QUEER

As a face at a bricked-up window,
Or the banging of a door in the desert,
This: 'Poking your nose in everywhere!'
'Me?' 'You — I give you warning:
''F I catch you in my dreams again,
'I'll break your neck next morning!'

★

Some things have to be believed to be seen.

★

. . . Such dreams as lay our being bare
And show us what we truly are —
           Bliss to wake from,
Even into the prison of care
           We sleep to break from.

★

I dreamed — alas, I only dreamed —
That things were other than they seemed . . .

★

A cracked, stained, old Inn ceiling
And an early cup of tea — and —
        All right, Michelangelo.

★

'I have been here before' —
I: I, my ancestor.

★

Did anyone ever have a boring dream?

THE RIDDLE

HE told himself and he told his wife,
His boy and his dog the Facts of Life.
Guess who'd known them all along;
Guess who'd found them in a song;
Guess who knew he'd got them wrong.

★

Have a care of the lad with a forelock
And a lass with a gipsying eye,
As you would of a witch or a warlock,
'F you wish to live single and die.

★

But Woman — in whose image made?

★

The soul's in the blood as the coal's in the wood.

★

The other woman in his life
Dropped out when she became his wife.

★

The fish looked bigger in the water.

★

The bad man, stepping on a beetle, hopes it hurts.

★

'Hell's gone to pot,' Satan said; 'there isn't one
of 'em above doing another a good turn on the sly.'

★

There's one thing to be said for sin —
It does give conscience exercise.

★

'Worm!' '*Glow*-worm!'

★

'Breeth,
'Bairns,
'Deeth,
'Cairns' —

As Malafont, Queen of Scotland, used to say.

★

When dandelions decked the Strand —
There's a poem!

Here's another :
Ships from Carthage putting in
At Market Jew with figs for tin —
Urgent in the wars with Rome —
And all the latest news from home.

And another:
When people sang God save the King —
Meaning royal Lud!

Still one more :
'*Lambert the marble cutter*' . . . (Survey of Stanhope,
County of Durham, in the Boldon Buke, 1183), *and, without a break in family or trade* : *from* Directory of Stanhope
(*Parson and White*), 1827:

  '*STONE MASONS*
  Gardner Whitfield
  Lambert John
  Robinson William
  Thompson George, etc.'

★

   The Golden Rule
Was called new-fangled, once upon a time.

★

Why not Fore*mothers*?

*

Poetrified — odd word.

*

'Poetaster!' 'Good: I'll twinkle in the sky.'

*

She died in her youth,
In her sleep: it would seem,
By the smile round her mouth,
In a beautiful dream.

*

Kitty and your thimble —
And all the jungles of Malay
Between the four legs of your chair . . .

*

The Muse consorts with whom she will —
Brought to bed and safely delivered,
She rises as the cord is severed:
Mother anew and maiden still.

*

'Had he been your father
'And she been your mother
'And you been another,
'Or not at all, rather —'
'*Eh?*'

*

Blessed are the children of a nobody.

*

. . . Thought in ruins, beautiful with ivy . . .

*

'Our forefathers fought
'A long, hard, bitter fight
'For Free Speech and Free Thought:
'Free Speech is our right.'

*

The handwriting on the wall may be a forgery.

*

'A spoonful of water contains a million billion
billion atoms — so I read!'
'A teaspoonful?'
'A tablespoonful.'
'Oh, *well*.'

*

He struck a light to see the stars —
And then mistook the moon for Mars!

*

The Movement, she explained, would bring
poetry to the rich.

*

How old is twenty? Ask Ten: ask Thirty:
ask Einstein.

*

The 'last word' is only the latest.

*

WHAT IS MAN . . ?

In the Void, those men of old —
Unless, indeed, they have been told —
Will change the tense a few years hence.

*

This is not a stupid joke : Anno Bombini.

*

Did a fallen nation ever
See its fall beforehand?

*

Big Six : Five : Four : Three : Two : Big —?

*

All that you will wish for *THEN*,
You lusty, active and untiring men,
Is sleep, and not to wake again.

*

'Last Days of Pomp . . .'

*

Only the Eskimo,
Staring at his dusty snow
Will ever know.

BIBLIOGRAPHICAL NOTE

The following note records the first publication of all the poems (arranged in alphabetical order of title) except those which first appeared in *The Last Blackbird and Other Lines* (1907), *Poems* (1917) and *The Skylark and Other Poems* (privately printed 1958). On later appearances several of these poems contained a few variations, not only in spelling and punctuation; in each case I have followed the author's most recent revision, together with a few minor changes in punctuation and spelling which he has requested me to make.

During the years 1944 to 1951 the author published eleven broadsheets or 'Flying Scrolls' (printed by Namleda and Company, Philadelphia) which consisted entirely of new poems. These are listed below, except certain of those untitled lines which appear between pages 168 and 178 in this volume.

All that you will wish for *Then*	'Flying Scroll', No. 6, 1947
Beauty Sprite	*The Saturday Review*, 23 February 1907
Beggar, The	*The Saturday Review*, 4 January 1908
Bride, The	*Today*, June 1921
Bull, The	*The Saturday Review*, 6 January 1912
Cardinal, The	*Silver Wedding and Other Poems*, Minerva, 1941
Churchill	'Flying Scroll', No. 3, 1945
Down by Moonlight, The	*The Saturday Review*, 22 July 1905
Epigram	*Silver Wedding and Other Poems*, Minerva, 1941
Eve	*The Saturday Review*, 3 February 1912

Ghoul Care	*The Saturday Review*, 29 July 1911
Gipsy Girl, The	*The Saturday Review*, 10 June 1911 (with one additional verse now omitted)
Hammers, The	*The Saturday Review*, 16 March 1907
Hever Picnic, The	'Flying Scroll', No. 1, 1944
Hymn to Moloch	*The Nation & Athenaeum*, 7 May 1921
I Love a Hill	*The Saturday Review*, 11 October 1913 (prefixed to 'The Song of Honour')
In Fancy Fair	*The Speaker*, 3 June 1905
Journeyman, The	*The Saturday Review*, 29 June 1907
Late, Last Rook, The	*The Saturday Review*, 27 April 1907 (with three additional verses now omitted)
Linnet, The	*The Saturday Review*, 24 March 1906 (under the title, 'The World')
Muse and the Mastiff, The	Selections from 'The Muse and the Mastiff: A Dramatic Poem', Part 1, Minerva 1941, and 'Flying Scrolls', Nos. 6, 7, 8, 9, 10, 11, 1947–1951
Night, The	*The Saturday Review*, 9 September 1905
Of Nature, write —	'Flying Scroll', No. 5, 1946
Old Words	*Silver Wedding and Other Poems*, Minerva, 1941
Ousel Cock' —, 'The	'Flying Scroll', No. 4, 1945
Pansy, The	*Silver Wedding and Other Poems*, Minerva, 1941
Peace, The	'Flying Scroll', No. 2, 1945
Playmates	*The Saturday Review*, 1 November 1913
Quarter-Day	*The Saturday Review*, 23 September 1905
Queer — Queer	'Flying Scroll', No. 4, 1945

C.F.

INDEX OF TITLES

('Flying Scrolls' do not appear in this Index unless they are
named in the Contents.)

INDEX OF FIRST LINES

('Flying Scrolls' do not appear in this Index unless they are named in the Contents.)

PRINTED IN GREAT BRITAIN
BY ROBERT MACLEHOSE AND CO. LTD
THE UNIVERSITY PRESS, GLASGOW